STM32 Programming G

First Edition
Sarful Hassan

Preface

This book is a comprehensive guide to programming STM32 microcontrollers. It provides detailed explanations, practical examples, and actionable tips to help developers of all levels. Whether you're a beginner exploring embedded systems or a seasoned developer looking to deepen your STM32 knowledge, this book has you covered.

Who This Book Is For

This book is intended for a wide range of audiences:

- Students learning STM32 for academic projects or research.
- Hobbyists interested in creating DIY projects with STM32 microcontrollers.
- Engineers building or optimizing STM32-based systems.
- Educators using STM32 as a tool to teach embedded systems concepts.
- Developers migrating to STM32 from other platforms or looking to advance their skills.

How This Book Is Organized

The book is divided into well-structured sections:

1. Introduction to STM32 microcontrollers and tools.
2. Input/Output (I/O) operations, including GPIO and advanced techniques.
3. Programming fundamentals like variables, data types, and control structures.
4. Advanced topics such as timers, math functions, and bitwise operations.
5. Practical examples for real-world applications.

Each chapter builds progressively, ensuring a seamless learning experience.

What Was Left Out

To maintain a focused and manageable scope, the following topics are not covered in-depth:

- Hardware design principles specific to STM32 boards.
- Non-STM32 specific peripheral modules.
- Advanced debugging, profiling, and optimization techniques.

For further exploration of these topics, readers can refer to the official STM32 documentation.

Code Style (About the Code)

All code examples in this book follow a clear and consistent style:

- Readable and thoroughly commented for better understanding.
- Applicable to various STM32 models.
- Tested on STM32 Nucleo and Discovery boards for accuracy.

We recommend using STM32CubeIDE or equivalent tools for the best development experience.

Release Notes

This updated edition includes:

- New examples on advanced topics like timers and bitwise operations.
- Enhanced beginner-friendly explanations.
- Content updated to reflect the latest STM32 development tools and libraries.

Notes on the First Edition

The first edition of this book laid the groundwork for learning STM32 programming. Based on valuable feedback from readers, this revised edition adds richer content and practical insights.

MechatronicsLAB Online Learning

For additional resources, tutorials, and support, visit MechatronicsLAB:
Email: mechatronicslab@gmail.com
Website: mechatronicslab.net

Acknowledgments for the First Edition

We would like to thank everyone who contributed to the success of this book, including the reviewers, testers, and the STM32 community.

Copyright

Disclaimer

Table of Contents

Introduction to STM32

Chapter Overview

STM32 microcontrollers, created by STMicroelectronics, are versatile, high-performance devices that find applications across a wide range of embedded systems. These microcontrollers balance computational power with energy efficiency, offer extensive peripheral support, and provide scalability across various models and series. This chapter introduces the STM32 family, explains its architecture and core features, guides readers on selecting the right STM32 model for specific applications, and covers essential development tools and software. It also provides an overview of ARM Cortex-M cores, which power STM32 microcontrollers.

Chapter Goal

- Understand the structure of the STM32 family and the application areas each series targets.
- Familiarize yourself with the STM32 architecture and key features that make it suitable for embedded applications.
- Learn criteria for choosing the right STM32 model for different projects.
- Explore the development tools and software used for STM32 programming, debugging, and testing.
- Gain foundational knowledge of ARM Cortex-M cores, which are the processing engines behind STM32 microcontrollers.

1. Overview of STM32 Family

STM32 microcontrollers are designed for flexibility, scalability, and efficiency, making them suitable for both simple and complex embedded applications. The STM32 family offers various series tailored to meet different application requirements, such as general-purpose, high-performance, low-power, and wireless connectivity.

Key Series in the STM32 Family

1. **STM32F Series - General-Purpose MCUs**
   - **Description**: The STM32F series is the most versatile in terms of performance and features, making it suitable for general-purpose applications.
   - **Key Features**: High-speed internal clocks, multiple ADC channels, large Flash memory options, and broad peripheral support.
   - **Subfamilies**:
     - **STM32F0**: Entry-level, low-cost series for basic control applications.
     - **STM32F1**: Widely used in various applications due to its balance of cost and performance.
     - **STM32F4**: High-performance series featuring ARM Cortex-M4 core with DSP capabilities.
     - **STM32F7**: Higher performance with the Cortex-M7 core, used in more demanding applications.
   - **Applications**: Industrial control, motor control, audio processing, and consumer electronics.

2. **STM32L Series - Low-Power MCUs**
   - **Description**: STM32L microcontrollers are designed with power-saving features to suit battery-operated and energy-sensitive applications.
   - **Key Features**: Ultra-low-power modes, multiple clock sources, and low-power peripherals.
   - **Subfamilies**:
     - **STM32L0 and L1**: Entry-level low-power series for simple IoT applications.
     - **STM32L4 and L5**: Higher performance with ARM Cortex-M4 and Cortex-M33 cores, suitable for more complex applications.
   - **Applications**: Wearables, environmental monitoring sensors, and portable medical devices.

3. **STM32H Series - High-Performance MCUs**
   - **Description**: The STM32H series is optimized for applications requiring intensive computational power.

- **Key Features**: Dual-core options, extensive memory, high-speed ADCs, and DSP capabilities.
- **Applications**: Real-time data processing, robotics, complex motor control, and automotive applications.

4. **STM32G Series - General-Purpose MCUs with Efficiency**
   - **Description**: Offers a balance between cost-efficiency and performance, with features tailored for cost-sensitive applications.
   - **Key Features**: Energy-efficient, broad peripheral support, and enhanced security features.
   - **Applications**: Consumer electronics, IoT devices, and general-purpose applications.

5. **STM32WB Series - Wireless MCUs**
   - **Description**: Integrated with Bluetooth and Zigbee connectivity, the STM32WB series is designed for wireless applications.
   - **Key Features**: Dual-core setup with ARM Cortex-M4 and Cortex-M0+ cores, optimized for wireless stacks and application processing.
   - **Applications**: Smart home devices, wearables, and connected sensors.

6. **STM32MP Series - Microprocessors with ARM Cortex-A**
   - **Description**: Combines ARM Cortex-A cores for high-level OS and Cortex-M cores for real-time processing.
   - **Key Features**: Supports Linux and real-time control, integrates advanced multimedia and connectivity features.
   - **Applications**: Industrial automation, control panels, and complex IoT applications requiring both real-time control and high-level OS.

STM32 Naming Convention

STM32 part numbers are structured to help identify the microcontroller series, performance level, and package type. A typical STM32 part number is structured as follows:

- **Prefix (STM32)**: Identifies the STM32 family.
- **Product Series (e.g., F4, L1)**: Denotes the series and subfamily (e.g., F4 for high-performance).
- **Memory Size, Pin Count, and Package**: Specifies details such as Flash memory, RAM, GPIO count, and package type (e.g., STM32F446RE has 512 KB Flash, 100 pins).

2. STM32 Architecture and Core Features

STM32 microcontrollers are built around ARM Cortex-M cores, offering low power consumption, high performance, and a rich set of peripherals to cater to a broad range of applications. The architecture of STM32 microcontrollers is optimized for embedded applications, combining efficient processing with powerful peripheral interfaces.

Key Features of STM32 Architecture

1. **ARM Cortex-M Cores**:
   - STM32 microcontrollers utilize ARM Cortex-M0, M0+, M3, M4, and M7 cores, each tailored to offer different levels of performance.
   - DSP capabilities in Cortex-M4 and M7 cores provide support for applications involving real-time data processing.
2. **Extensive Peripheral Support**:
   - STM32 MCUs integrate a variety of peripherals such as ADC, DAC, PWM, UART, SPI, I2C, and CAN, enabling seamless interfacing with sensors, actuators, and external memory.
   - Specialized peripherals, like USB, Ethernet, and SDIO, support more complex connectivity requirements.
3. **High-Speed Memory and Flash Options**:
   - STM32 microcontrollers offer up to 2MB of Flash memory, with options for external memory support (NOR, NAND, and SDRAM).

o   Configurable memory architecture allows for data and code separation, enhancing performance.
4. **Advanced Power Management**:
      o   Multiple power-saving modes (Sleep, Stop, Standby) provide flexibility in managing power consumption.
      o   Designed to accommodate battery-operated applications through advanced power control.
5. **Enhanced Security**:
      o   Certain STM32 models include security features like secure boot, cryptographic accelerators, and memory protection, suitable for IoT and secure communication.
6. **Flexible Clock Configuration**:
      o   Configurable clock sources and clock dividers allow customization of CPU and peripheral speeds, optimizing both performance and power usage.

Core Components of STM32 MCUs

- **CPU (Central Processing Unit)**: ARM Cortex-M cores provide the necessary processing power for embedded applications, with support for efficient task management and DSP.
- **Memory Architecture**: On-chip Flash and SRAM, alongside external memory support, allow STM32 MCUs to handle large data and complex code requirements.
- **System Peripherals**:
      o   **GPIO**: Allows control of input and output signals.
      o   **Timers**: Provides accurate time-keeping, PWM generation, and event handling.
      o   **Analog Peripherals**: ADC and DAC channels support analog signal processing.

3. Choosing the Right STM32 Model

Selecting the right STM32 microcontroller involves evaluating factors like performance, memory, power requirements, and peripheral support. Different STM32 series cater to specific applications and project requirements.

Application-Based Model Selection

1. **Basic Control Applications (Entry-Level)**:
   - ○ **Suggested Series**: STM32F0, STM32G0
   - ○ **Typical Applications**: Home automation, basic IoT devices, simple motor control.
   - ○ **Considerations**: Opt for lower-cost models with essential peripherals.
2. **Battery-Powered and Low-Power Applications**:
   - ○ **Suggested Series**: STM32L series
   - ○ **Typical Applications**: Wearable devices, environmental sensors, battery-operated devices.
   - ○ **Considerations**: Focus on models with ultra-low-power modes and energy-efficient peripherals.
3. **High-Performance and DSP Applications**:
   - ○ **Suggested Series**: STM32F4, STM32F7, STM32H7
   - ○ **Typical Applications**: Industrial automation, robotics, data processing.
   - ○ **Considerations**: Prioritize processing power, memory, and advanced peripherals.
4. **Wireless IoT Applications**:
   - ○ **Suggested Series**: STM32WB
   - ○ **Typical Applications**: Smart home systems, Bluetooth-enabled wearables.
   - ○ **Considerations**: Ensure compatibility with Bluetooth or Zigbee wireless protocols.
5. **Embedded Systems with Real-Time OS Requirements**:
   - ○ **Suggested Series**: STM32MP1 series
   - ○ **Typical Applications**: Systems requiring both high-level OS and real-time control, such as industrial HMI panels.
   - ○ **Considerations**: Requires a dual-core setup to handle both Linux OS tasks and real-time processing.

Considerations for Model Selection

- **Required Peripherals**: Match the MCU's peripherals with project needs (e.g., ADC, DAC, communication protocols).
- **Power Consumption**: Low-power models should be prioritized for battery-dependent projects.

- **Memory Requirements**: Choose a model with sufficient Flash and RAM to handle the application code and data.
- **Cost Constraints**: Ensure the selected model aligns with the project's budget.

4. Development Tools and Software

STM32 microcontrollers are supported by a range of development environments and tools. The primary tool recommended for STM32 development is STM32CubeIDE, but others like Keil and IAR are popular in commercial applications.

STM32CubeIDE

- **Overview**: STM32CubeIDE is an integrated development environment that combines the graphical configuration of STM32CubeMX with the Eclipse IDE, providing a complete tool for STM32 development.
- **Key Features**:
  - Supports STM32CubeMX for hardware configuration.
  - Integrated editor, compiler, and debugger.
  - Extensive debugging capabilities using STM32 debuggers.
- **Use Case**: Ideal for both beginners and advanced users, offering a complete solution for setting up, configuring, and debugging STM32 projects.

STM32CubeMX

- **Overview**: STM32CubeMX is a configuration tool that simplifies hardware setup by allowing users to visually configure the MCU's peripherals, pins, and clock tree.
- **Key Features**:
  - Graphical configuration of GPIO, peripherals, and clocks.
  - Generates initialization code for STM32 projects.
- **Use Case**: Essential for configuring the microcontroller's hardware setup before coding.

Keil MDK-ARM

- **Overview**: A professional IDE optimized for ARM Cortex-M microcontrollers, featuring a highly efficient compiler and extensive debugging capabilities.
- **Key Features**:
  - Optimized compiler for ARM, with real-time operating system (RTOS) support.
  - Debugging tools with real-time performance monitoring.
- **Use Case**: Suitable for commercial projects that require code optimization and professional debugging tools.

IAR Embedded Workbench

- **Overview**: Another high-performance IDE that offers a robust compiler and advanced debugging tools for embedded development.
- **Key Features**:
  - Advanced code profiling and power debugging capabilities.
- **Use Case**: Ideal for projects needing highly optimized code and complex debugging.

Other Tools

- **STM32 ST-LINK Utility**: Flashing and debugging tool for STM32 firmware.
- **STM32CubeProgrammer**: For flashing, debugging, and firmware upgrades, supporting wired and wireless updates.

5. Introduction to ARM Cortex-M Cores

STM32 microcontrollers are powered by ARM Cortex-M cores, which are designed specifically for embedded applications, providing efficient processing with low power consumption and real-time capability.

Overview of ARM Cortex-M Cores

1. **Cortex-M0 and M0+**:
   - Entry-level cores with basic features, optimized for low-power applications.
   - Suitable for cost-sensitive, low-power projects.
2. **Cortex-M3**:
   - Mid-range performance with improved efficiency and integrated debugging capabilities.
   - Common in general-purpose applications.
3. **Cortex-M4**:
   - Adds DSP (Digital Signal Processing) capabilities for applications requiring signal processing.
   - Used in applications like motor control, sensor data processing, and audio processing.
4. **Cortex-M7**:
   - High-performance core with both DSP and FPU (Floating Point Unit) for intensive applications.
   - Suitable for robotics, real-time processing, and high-speed data acquisition.
5. **Cortex-A (STM32MP Series)**:
   - Supports high-level OS like Linux, with Cortex-M cores handling real-time control.
   - Suitable for advanced systems needing a combination of real-time control and OS functions.

6 Core Features of ARM Cortex-M Cores

- **Efficient Interrupt Handling**: NVIC (Nested Vector Interrupt Controller) ensures low-latency response for real-time applications.
- **Debugging Support**: Built-in support for debugging with SWD (Serial Wire Debug) and JTAG.
- **Memory Protection Unit (MPU)**: Enhances application security and stability by segmenting memory access.
- **FPU**: Enables efficient handling of floating-point operations on Cortex-M4 and M7 cores.
- **DSP Extensions**: Supports data processing and manipulation, crucial for signal processing applications.

STM32 Nucleo-F401RE Development Board Guid

The STM32 Nucleo-F401RE is a highly versatile development board designed for prototyping with the STM32F401RET6 microcontroller, a member of the ARM Cortex-M4 family. It combines robust performance, power efficiency, and flexibility, making it ideal for embedded systems, IoT, and robotics projects.

- **Key Advantages**:
  - Compatible with Arduino UNO R3 shields.
  - Extended functionality with STM32 Morpho headers.
  - Integrated ST-LINK/V2-1 for seamless debugging and programming.

Key Features

1. **Microcontroller**: STM32F401RET6
   - 32-bit ARM Cortex-M4 processor with a Floating Point Unit (FPU).
   - Operates at a clock speed of 84 MHz.
2. **Memory**:
   - 512 KB Flash Memory for program storage.
   - 96 KB SRAM for efficient data handling.
3. **Power Supply**:
   - Operates at 3.3V internally.
   - Supports external input voltage of 7V-12V via VIN.
   - USB-powered with an onboard voltage regulator.
4. **Onboard Debugger**: Integrated ST-LINK/V2-1 supporting SWD and JTAG protocols.
5. **Pin Compatibility**:
   - Arduino UNO R3 headers for shield integration.
   - STM32 Morpho headers for access to all GPIOs and peripherals.
6. **LEDs and Buttons**:
   - **LD1**: USB communication indicator.
   - **LD2**: User-programmable LED.
   - **LD3**: Power indicator.
   - Two Push Buttons: One for reset and another for user control.

Pinout Configuration

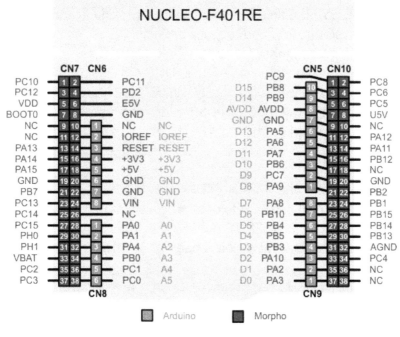

NUCLEO-F401RE

1. Arduino-Compatible Headers
- Provides compatibility with Arduino shields.
- Divided into four categories: CN5, CN6, CN8, CN9.

Category	Pin Type	Pin Names	Description
CN6 (Power)	Reference Voltage	IOREF	3.3V reference voltage pin for shields.
	Reset	RESET	Resets the microcontroller.
	Power Output	+3.3V, +5V	Provides 3.3V and 5V output.
	Ground	GND	System ground pins.

CN8 (Analog)	Analog Input Pins	A0, A1	Analog pins for voltage measurement (12-bit ADC).
	I2C Communication	A4 (SDA), A5 (SCL)	I2C communication pins.
CN5 (Digital)	Digital GPIO Pins	D8-D15	General-purpose digital input/output pins.
	SPI Communication	D10 (CS), D11 (MOSI), D12 (MISO), D13 (SCK)	SPI communication.
CN9 (USART)	Digital GPIO Pins	D0-D7	Digital GPIO pins.
	UART Communication	D0 (Rx), D1 (Tx)	UART/USART communication pins.

2. STM32 Morpho Headers

- Two rows of male headers (CN7 and CN10) provide access to extended GPIOs and peripherals.

Category	Pin Type	Pin Names	Description
CN7	GPIO Pins	PC0-PC3, PC10-PC15, PA0-PA15	General-purpose GPIO pins for peripherals.
	Power	VBAT, +3.3V, +5V, VIN	Power input/output pins.

	Reset	RESET	Resets the microcontroller.
	Reference Voltage	IOREF	3.3V reference voltage.
CN10	GPIO Pins	PA2-PA12, PB1-PB15, PC4-PC9	Additional GPIO pins.
	Power	U5V, GND, AGND	Power and ground pins.

Technical Specifications

Feature	Details
Microcontroller	STM32F401RET6 (ARM Cortex M4)
Architecture	ARM Cortex M4 with Floating Point Unit (FPU)
Clock Speed	84 MHz
Memory	512 KB Flash, 96 KB SRAM
GPIO Pins	50
ADC	12-bit, 16 channels
Timers	16-bit (6), 32-bit (2)
Communication Interfaces	4x USART/UART, 3x I2C, 3x SPI
USB Support	USB 2.0 Full-Speed

RTC	Integrated 32kHz oscillator with calibration
Power Input	7V-15V (VIN), USB-powered
Operating Voltage	1.7V-3.6V (MCU), 3.3V system
Power Consumption	2.4 µA (standby without RTC)
Crystal Oscillators	Internal (16 MHz), External (4-26 MHz)
Onboard Debugger	ST-LINK/V2-1, supports SWD and JTAG

Hardware Details
1. **Microcontroller: STM32F401RET6**
   - High-performance ARM Cortex-M4 core.
   - Supports complex mathematical operations with its Floating Point Unit (FPU).
   - Low power consumption for efficient applications.
2. **Arduino Compatibility**
   - Pinout matches Arduino UNO R3, making it easy to use existing Arduino shields.
   - Simplifies development for users transitioning from Arduino to STM32.
3. **STM32 Morpho Headers**
   - Provides access to all the microcontroller's GPIOs and peripherals.
   - Useful for advanced projects requiring additional functionality.
4. **Integrated Debugger**
   - ST-LINK/V2-1 allows for debugging and programming without external hardware.
   - Supports firmware upgrade for added features.
5. **LEDs and Buttons**
   - LEDs:
     - **LD1**: USB communication activity.

- **LD2**: Programmable for user-defined functions.
- **LD3**: Power indication.
    - Buttons:
        - User button for custom input.
        - Reset button for restarting the MCU.

Power Supply Options
- **USB Powered**: Connect via a micro-USB cable for 5V input.
- **VIN Pin**: External power supply (7V-12V recommended, up to 15V).
- **3.3V Pin**: Directly power the MCU using a regulated 3.3V input.
- **Battery Power**: Connect a coin cell battery to VBAT for RTC functionality.

Performance Highlights
- **Speed and Efficiency**: With an 84 MHz clock and advanced peripherals, the STM32 Nucleo-F401RE offers superior performance compared to many 8-bit development boards.
- **Versatility**: Combines Arduino compatibility with advanced STM32 features for a wide range of applications.
- **Debugging Capability**: Built-in ST-LINK debugger supports real-time debugging and step-through code execution.

Getting Started with STM32

Chapter Overview

Getting started with STM32 development requires understanding the tools, software, and steps necessary to set up a functioning development environment. This chapter will guide you through setting up STM32CubeIDE, using STM32CubeMX to configure hardware, flashing programs onto the microcontroller, setting up projects, and performing basic debugging. By the end of this chapter, you will be equipped with the foundational skills to start building STM32-based applications.

Chapter Goal

- Successfully set up the STM32 development environment on your computer.
- Learn to use STM32CubeMX for configuring peripherals, pins, and clocks.
- Understand the process of flashing compiled code onto an STM32 microcontroller.
- Navigate STM32CubeIDE for project setup, code management, and building projects.
- Acquire basic debugging techniques to test and troubleshoot embedded applications.

1. Setting up the Development Environment

To develop applications for STM32 microcontrollers, you'll need to install specific tools and software, as well as set up the necessary hardware. Here's a step-by-step guide to ensure you're prepared to start coding.

Required Software and Tools

1. **STM32CubeIDE**:
   - **Description**: STM32CubeIDE is an all-in-one integrated development environment (IDE) that combines code editing, compiling, debugging, and hardware configuration using STM32CubeMX.
   - **Features**:
     - Built-in STM32CubeMX for graphical hardware configuration.
     - Code editor with syntax highlighting, code suggestions, and error detection.
     - Integrated compiler and debugger for seamless code development.
   - **Installation**:
     - Download STM32CubeIDE from the STMicroelectronics website.
     - Follow the installation wizard, choosing installation options based on your operating system (Windows, macOS, or Linux).
     - Open STM32CubeIDE after installation to confirm it's working properly.
2. **STM32CubeMX**:
   - **Description**: STM32CubeMX is a configuration and code-generation tool used for setting up microcontroller peripherals, clocks, and pin assignments.
   - **Standalone vs. Integrated**: STM32CubeMX is integrated within STM32CubeIDE, but a standalone version is also available.
   - **Installation**: If you're using STM32CubeIDE, STM32CubeMX is already included, so no additional installation is required.
3. **ST-LINK/V2 or ST-LINK/V3 Debugger**:
   - **Purpose**: The ST-LINK hardware debugging tool is used to flash (program) and debug STM32 microcontrollers.

- ○ **Connection**: Connects via USB to your computer and to the STM32 development board via the SWD (Serial Wire Debug) interface or JTAG.
4. **ST-LINK USB Driver (for Windows users)**:
   - ○ **Purpose**: The ST-LINK USB driver allows Windows to recognize and communicate with the ST-LINK debugger.
   - ○ **Installation**: Download the ST-LINK USB driver from the STMicroelectronics website and install it following the provided instructions.

Development Hardware

1. **STM32 Development Board**: Common boards include STM32 Nucleo, Discovery, and Evaluation boards. Select a board that meets your project requirements (e.g., STM32F446RE Nucleo).
2. **USB Cable**: A USB cable connects the STM32 board to your computer for power, flashing, and debugging.

Verifying Installation and Setup

1. **Open STM32CubeIDE**: Launch STM32CubeIDE to ensure it opens without issues.
2. **Connect the STM32 Board**: Connect your STM32 development board to the computer via USB.
3. **Check for Device Detection**: In STM32CubeIDE, verify that the board is detected by checking the **Run** or **Debug** configurations. The board should appear in the list with its device name and serial number.

2. STM32CubeMX: Code Generation and Configuration

STM32CubeMX is a powerful graphical tool used for configuring the hardware settings of STM32 microcontrollers. Using STM32CubeMX, you can set up peripherals, configure GPIO pins, adjust clock settings, and generate initialization code that STM32CubeIDE uses.

Steps for Using STM32CubeMX

1. **Create a New Project**:
   - Open STM32CubeIDE and navigate to **File > New > STM32 Project**.
   - In the **Target Selection** window, select your STM32 model. You can filter by series (e.g., STM32F4) or directly search by part number (e.g., STM32F103C8).
   - Select the desired microcontroller, click **Next**, and enter the project name, location, and toolchain (STM32CubeIDE).

2. **Configure GPIO Pins and Peripherals**:
   - In the graphical interface, click on pins to assign specific functions (e.g., GPIO, UART, I2C, ADC).
   - Each peripheral will offer adjustable settings. For example:
     - **GPIO**: Set pins as input, output, or alternate function.
     - **UART**: Configure TX/RX pins and set baud rate.
     - **I2C and SPI**: Set clock speed and choose appropriate pins.

3. **Configure the Clock**:
   - Open the **Clock Configuration** tab to set up system and peripheral clocks.
   - Select an internal (HSI) or external (HSE) clock source, and adjust prescalers and dividers.
   - Configure the clock frequency for the core and buses (AHB, APB1, and APB2).

4. **Set Middleware Options** (Optional):
   - In the **Middleware** tab, enable libraries like FreeRTOS (for real-time OS), USB, or FATFS (for file systems).
   - Set up middleware parameters if your project requires advanced features like USB or RTOS.

5. **Generate Code**:
   - After completing the setup, click on **Project > Generate Code**.

- STM32CubeMX will generate initialization code based on the configured peripherals, including HAL (Hardware Abstraction Layer) library setup.
- The generated code includes `main.c`, peripheral initialization functions, and other project files required to start coding.

Understanding the Generated Code Structure

- **main.c**: The main file containing the core application logic and the main loop.
- **stm32xxxx_hal_conf.h**: Configuration file that enables or disables HAL modules.
- **Drivers folder**: Contains peripheral drivers and STM32 HAL libraries.
- **system_stm32xxxx.c**: Sets up system clocks and resets.

The code generated by STM32CubeMX ensures the initial setup is ready for use, enabling developers to focus on building their application without manual configuration.

3. Flashing Programs to STM32 Microcontrollers

Flashing a program to an STM32 microcontroller involves transferring the compiled binary to the microcontroller's memory, enabling it to execute the code. STM32CubeIDE simplifies the flashing process using the built-in ST-LINK debugger.

Steps for Flashing Programs

1. **Build the Project**:
   - In STM32CubeIDE, click **Project > Build Project** or click the **Build** button.
   - This compiles the code and generates a binary file (.bin or .hex) ready for flashing.
   - Review the **Console** output for any errors or warnings.

2. **Set Up Flash Settings**:
   - Ensure the STM32 board is connected to your computer via the ST-LINK debugger.
   - In STM32CubeIDE, go to **Run > Debug Configurations** to open the configuration settings.
   - Select **ST-LINK** as the debug probe and check that the correct microcontroller model is detected.
3. **Flash the Code to the STM32 Microcontroller**:
   - Click **Debug** (or **Run** if debugging isn't required).
   - STM32CubeIDE will erase the current flash memory, write the new binary file, and start executing the program.
   - Upon successful flashing, the program will automatically start running on the microcontroller.

Verifying Program Execution

- **LED or Output**: If your program involves LEDs, verify that the behavior matches the expected output.
- **Serial Output**: For programs using UART, open a serial terminal (e.g., PuTTY) to monitor the output from the STM32.

4. Using STM32CubeIDE for Project Setup

STM32CubeIDE serves as the primary workspace for code development, offering an integrated environment for managing code files, building projects, and debugging.

Creating and Managing a Project in STM32CubeIDE

1. **Starting a New Project**:
   - Open STM32CubeIDE and go to **File > New > STM32 Project**.
   - Select the STM32 microcontroller you are using, give the project a name, choose the location, and finish setup.

2. **Editing Code**:
   - ○ STM32CubeIDE provides syntax highlighting, code suggestions, and error checking, making it easier to code efficiently.
   - ○ Write custom functions and application logic in the `main.c` file, under the main loop or as separate functions.
3. **Building the Project**:
   - ○ Build the project by clicking **Project > Build All** or using the **Build** icon.
   - ○ Compilation messages will appear in the **Console** and **Problems** tabs, highlighting any errors or warnings.
4. **Setting Up Build and Debug Configurations**:
   - ○ Open **Project Properties** to configure compiler settings, including optimization levels and linker settings.
   - ○ In **Debug Configurations**, confirm that the debug probe is set to **ST-LINK** and the correct microcontroller is selected.

Understanding Key Project Files

- **main.c**: The core file containing the main loop where most application code is written.
- **stm32xxxx_hal_conf.h**: Configuration file that controls which HAL modules are enabled.
- **system_stm32xxxx.c**: Configures system initialization, including setting up clocks and interrupts.
- **Drivers folder**: Contains the HAL libraries for each peripheral and the CMSIS (Cortex Microcontroller Software Interface Standard) files.

5. Debugging Basics

Debugging is an essential skill in embedded programming, allowing you to locate and fix issues in your code. STM32CubeIDE provides powerful debugging tools, including breakpoints, variable inspection, and step-through execution.

Setting Up Debugging

1. **Connect the ST-LINK Debugger**:
   - Make sure the ST-LINK debugger is connected to both the computer and the STM32 development board.
   - In STM32CubeIDE, open **Debug Configurations** and confirm that the ST-LINK debugger is selected.
2. **Starting a Debugging Session**:
   - Click **Debug** to start a debugging session.
   - STM32CubeIDE will build the project, flash the code to the board, and halt execution at the beginning of `main()`.
3. **Using Breakpoints**:
   - Set breakpoints by clicking on the left margin next to the line number in `main.c`.
   - Breakpoints stop the code execution at specified points, allowing you to inspect program variables and states.
4. **Step-Through Execution**:
   - **Step Into**: Steps into the function call to debug line-by-line.
   - **Step Over**: Executes the current line and moves to the next without entering functions.
   - **Step Out**: Completes the current function and returns to the caller.
5. **Inspecting Variables and Expressions**:
   - Use the **Variables** tab to monitor and modify variable values at runtime.
   - Add specific expressions in the **Expressions** tab to track variable changes or expressions during program execution.
6. **Debug Console**:
   - The console provides real-time information on program execution, error messages, and debugging insights.
   - **Using Watches**: Add watches for key variables to track their values in real time.

Introduction to GPIO

Chapter Overview

GPIO (General-Purpose Input/Output) is a fundamental feature of microcontrollers, enabling interaction with external components like LEDs, buttons, sensors, and relays. STM32 microcontrollers offer flexible GPIO configurations, allowing each pin to be set as input, output, analog, or an alternate function. This chapter will cover the basics of GPIO, how to configure GPIO pins in STM32CubeMX, different GPIO modes, and practical examples for input and output.

Chapter Goal

- Understand the GPIO architecture and functions in STM32 microcontrollers.
- Learn to configure GPIO pins as input and output.
- Explore different GPIO modes and their applications.
- Implement basic input and output examples, such as controlling an LED and reading a button state.

1. GPIO Overview in STM32

GPIO (General-Purpose Input/Output) pins provide digital input and output capabilities, allowing microcontrollers to interface with other digital components. Each GPIO pin can be configured to perform different roles such as input, output, or to act as an alternate function (e.g., UART, SPI, I2C).

GPIO Port and Pin Structure

- **Ports**: STM32 microcontrollers organize GPIO pins into ports, typically labeled as **GPIOA**, **GPIOB**, **GPIOC**, etc. Each port can have up to 16 pins.
- **Pins**: Each port pin is numbered from 0 to 15 (e.g., PA0, PB5, PC13).

- **Multipurpose Functionality**: Each pin can be set to a different mode, such as digital input, digital output, analog, or alternate function for peripherals.

GPIO Pin Modes in STM32

1. **Input Mode**:
   - Used to read a digital state (high or low) from an external source, like a button.
2. **Output Mode**:
   - Used to send digital signals to external devices, like turning an LED on or off.
3. **Alternate Function Mode**:
   - Enables the pin to serve as an input/output for internal peripherals, such as UART, SPI, I2C.
4. **Analog Mode**:
   - Configures the pin for analog input/output, typically for ADC (Analog-to-Digital Converter) or DAC (Digital-to-Analog Converter).

GPIO Speed, Pull-Up, and Pull-Down

- **Speed**: Controls the speed at which a pin can toggle between high and low (Low, Medium, High, or Very High speed). Faster speeds consume more power but are essential for high-frequency signals.
- **Pull-Up/Pull-Down Resistors**: Internal resistors can be configured as pull-up, pull-down, or none. Pull-up resistors set the default state to high when no external signal is connected, while pull-down resistors set it to low.

2. Configuring GPIO with STM32CubeMX

STM32CubeMX is used to configure GPIO pins in a graphical interface, simplifying the setup process. You can assign each pin's function, mode, pull-up/pull-down state, and speed.

Steps to Configure GPIO Pins

1. **Open STM32CubeMX and Create a New Project**:
   - Start STM32CubeIDE or the standalone STM32CubeMX tool.
   - Select your microcontroller model or board (e.g., STM32F103C8T6 or Nucleo-F446RE) to create a new project.
2. **Assign Pin Functions**:
   - Click on each pin in the graphical interface to configure it.
   - Choose **GPIO_Output** for output pins (e.g., controlling an LED) or **GPIO_Input** for input pins (e.g., reading a button).
3. **Configure GPIO Parameters**:
   - **Mode**: Select `Input`, `Output`, `Analog`, or `Alternate Function`.
   - **Pull-Up/Pull-Down**: Choose between No Pull, Pull-Up, or Pull-Down resistor options.
   - **Speed**: Set Low, Medium, High, or Very High speed depending on the application.
4. **Generate Code**:
   - Click **Project > Generate Code** to create initialization code for the configured GPIO pins.
   - STM32CubeMX will generate code files that include initialization functions for each GPIO pin.

Understanding GPIO Initialization Code in main.c

The generated code in `main.c` contains functions and macros to initialize and control GPIO pins. Here's an example of typical GPIO initialization code:

```
void MX_GPIO_Init(void) {
    GPIO_InitTypeDef GPIO_InitStruct = {0};

    /* Enable GPIO Clock */
    __HAL_RCC_GPIOA_CLK_ENABLE();
    __HAL_RCC_GPIOB_CLK_ENABLE();

    /* Configure GPIO pin as output */
    GPIO_InitStruct.Pin = GPIO_PIN_5;
```

```
GPIO_InitStruct.Mode = GPIO_MODE_OUTPUT_PP;
GPIO_InitStruct.Pull = GPIO_NOPULL;
GPIO_InitStruct.Speed = GPIO_SPEED_FREQ_LOW;
HAL_GPIO_Init(GPIOA, &GPIO_InitStruct);

/* Configure GPIO pin as input */
GPIO_InitStruct.Pin = GPIO_PIN_13;
GPIO_InitStruct.Mode = GPIO_MODE_INPUT;
GPIO_InitStruct.Pull = GPIO_PULLUP;
HAL_GPIO_Init(GPIOC, &GPIO_InitStruct);
}
```

- **Clock Enable**: Enables the clock for GPIOA and GPIOC, allowing those ports to be used.
- **GPIO Initialization**: Configures the pins with specified modes, pull-up/pull-down resistors, and speed.

3. Using GPIO for Output

GPIO output mode allows the STM32 microcontroller to control external devices by setting a pin to a high or low state. For example, controlling an LED involves setting a GPIO pin high to turn it on and low to turn it off.

Example: Blinking an LED

This example demonstrates how to blink an LED using GPIO in output mode.

1. **Hardware Setup**:
    - Connect an LED to GPIOA pin PA5, with a current-limiting resistor (e.g., 220Ω) between the LED and the pin.
2. **GPIO Configuration in STM32CubeMX**:
    - Set PA5 as **GPIO_Output** in STM32CubeMX.
    - Configure the pin as Output mode, with No Pull and Low Speed.
3. **Code Example for LED Blinking**:

```
#include "main.h"

int main(void) {
    HAL_Init();
    MX_GPIO_Init();  // Initializes GPIO configurations

    while (1) {
        HAL_GPIO_WritePin(GPIOA, GPIO_PIN_5, GPIO_PIN_SET);   // Turn on
LED
        HAL_Delay(500);                                        // Delay
500 ms
        HAL_GPIO_WritePin(GPIOA, GPIO_PIN_5, GPIO_PIN_RESET);  // Turn
off LED
        HAL_Delay(500);                                        // Delay
500 ms
    }
}
```

Explanation of the Code

- **HAL_GPIO_WritePin**: Sets GPIOA pin 5 high (GPIO_PIN_SET) to turn on the LED and low (GPIO_PIN_RESET) to turn it off.
- **HAL_Delay**: Creates a delay of 500 milliseconds between each state change, resulting in a blinking effect.

4. Using GPIO for Input

GPIO input mode allows the STM32 microcontroller to read digital signals from external devices, such as switches, buttons, and sensors.

Example: Reading a Button State

In this example, we configure a GPIO pin to detect whether a button is pressed or released.

1. **Hardware Setup**:
   o Connect a push-button to GPIOC pin PC13, with one terminal connected to ground and the other connected to PC13. Ensure the pin has an internal pull-up resistor enabled.

2. **GPIO Configuration in STM32CubeMX**:
    - Set PC13 as **GPIO_Input**.
    - Configure the pin mode as `Input`, with a `Pull-Up` resistor to ensure a default high state when the button is not pressed.
3. **Code Example for Button Input**:

```c
#include "main.h"

int main(void) {
    HAL_Init();
    MX_GPIO_Init();  // Initializes GPIO configurations

    while (1) {
        if (HAL_GPIO_ReadPin(GPIOC, GPIO_PIN_13) == GPIO_PIN_RESET) {
            // Button pressed
            HAL_GPIO_WritePin(GPIOA, GPIO_PIN_5, GPIO_PIN_SET);  //
Turn on LED
        } else {
            // Button released
            HAL_GPIO_WritePin(GPIOA, GPIO_PIN_5, GPIO_PIN_RESET);  //
Turn off LED
        }
    }
}
```

Explanation of the Code

- **HAL_GPIO_ReadPin**: Reads the state of GPIOC pin 13. When the button is pressed, the pin state is low (GPIO_PIN_RESET), otherwise, it is high (GPIO_PIN_SET).
- **If-Else Statement**: If the button is pressed, the LED turns on. If released, the LED turns off.

5. GPIO Interrupts

GPIO interrupts allow the STM32 microcontroller to respond to changes in a GPIO pin state (e.g., when a button is pressed). Interrupts enable efficient processing, as they allow the MCU to react to events immediately without constant polling.

Setting Up a GPIO Interrupt

1. **Configure the Pin for Interrupt in STM32CubeMX**:
    - Set PC13 as **GPIO_Input** with `Pull-Up`.

- ○ Enable **EXTI Line 13** interrupt for PC13 in the NVIC settings.
2. **Code Example for Button Interrupt**:

```
#include "main.h"

void HAL_GPIO_EXTI_Callback(uint16_t GPIO_Pin) {
    if (GPIO_Pin == GPIO_PIN_13) {
        HAL_GPIO_TogglePin(GPIOA, GPIO_PIN_5);  // Toggle LED
    }
}

int main(void) {
    HAL_Init();
    MX_GPIO_Init();  // Initializes GPIO configurations

    while (1) {
        // Main loop can perform other tasks
    }
}
```

Explanation of the Code

- **HAL_GPIO_EXTI_Callback**: A callback function triggered by an interrupt on PC13. It checks if the interrupt is from GPIO_PIN_13 and toggles the LED accordingly.
- **Toggle LED**: HAL_GPIO_TogglePin changes the LED state each time the button is pressed.

---

6. GPIO Pull-Up and Pull-Down Resistors

Internal pull-up and pull-down resistors help maintain a stable logic level (high or low) on GPIO input pins when there's no external connection. This is essential for stable signal reading, especially with buttons and switches.

Types of Resistors

- **Pull-Up Resistor**: Keeps the pin at a high logic level (Vcc) when no input signal is present.
- **Pull-Down Resistor**: Keeps the pin at a low logic level (ground) when no input signal is present.

Digital I/O in STM32

Chapter Overview

Digital I/O (Input/Output) functionality is fundamental in embedded systems, enabling microcontrollers to interact with external components like LEDs, switches, sensors, and relays. The STM32 NUCLEO-F446RE provides General Purpose Input/Output (GPIO) pins that can be configured as digital inputs or outputs. This chapter covers GPIO configurations and demonstrates practical usage in a final project.

Chapter Goal

- Learn how to configure GPIO pins as digital inputs and outputs on the STM32 NUCLEO-F446RE.
- Understand how to control external components, such as LEDs, using GPIO outputs.
- Learn to read signals from components, like buttons, using GPIO inputs.
- Complete a hands-on project to toggle an LED based on button presses, demonstrating practical GPIO usage.

Rules

- **Enable GPIO Clock**: Enable the clock for each GPIO port before configuring pins to power the port.
- **Set Pin Mode**: Define each pin as input, output, or alternate function.
- **Use Pull-Up/Down Resistors**: Configure internal pull-up or pull-down resistors to stabilize input signals and avoid floating inputs.
- **Output Control**: Use GPIO output to control external devices.
- **Input Reading**: Set GPIO pins as inputs to read external signals.

Syntax Table

Serial No	Topic	Code Snippet	Simple Example
1	Enable GPIO Clock	`__HAL_RCC_GPIOx_CLK_ENABLE()`	`__HAL_RCC_GPIOA_CLK_ENABLE()`
2	Configure GPIO Pin Mode	`GPIO_InitStruct.Mode = GPIO_MODE_xxx`	`GPIO_InitStruct.Mode = GPIO_MODE_OUTPUT_PP`
3	Configure GPIO Speed	`GPIO_InitStruct.Speed = GPIO_SPEED_xxx`	`GPIO_InitStruct.Speed = GPIO_SPEED_LOW`
4	Set Output High	`HAL_GPIO_WritePin(GPIOx, GPIO_PIN_y, GPIO_PIN_SET)`	`HAL_GPIO_WritePin(GPIOA, GPIO_PIN_5, GPIO_PIN_SET)`
5	Set Output Low	`HAL_GPIO_WritePin(GPIOx, GPIO_PIN_y, GPIO_PIN_RESET)`	`HAL_GPIO_WritePin(GPIOA, GPIO_PIN_5, GPIO_PIN_RESET)`
6	Toggle GPIO Pin	`HAL_GPIO_TogglePin(GPIOx, GPIO_PIN_y)`	`HAL_GPIO_TogglePin(GPIOA, GPIO_PIN_5)`
7	Read GPIO Input	`HAL_GPIO_ReadPin(GPIOx, GPIO_PIN_y)`	`HAL_GPIO_ReadPin(GPIOB, GPIO_PIN_0)`

Topic Explanations

1. Enable GPIO Clock

What is Enabling the GPIO Clock?

Enabling the GPIO clock provides power to a GPIO port, making the port's pins accessible for configuration and use. Without enabling the clock, any operations on the port will be ineffective.

Use Purpose

- **Activate GPIO Ports**: Powers the selected GPIO port (e.g., GPIOA, GPIOB) to make it operational.
- **Essential for GPIO Operations**: Enables communication and configuration of GPIO pins.

Syntax

```
__HAL_RCC_GPIOx_CLK_ENABLE();
```

Syntax Explanation

- **__HAL_RCC**: Prefix used in STM32 HAL (Hardware Abstraction Layer) functions related to Reset and Clock Control (RCC).
- **GPIOx**: Specifies the GPIO port to enable, such as GPIOA, GPIOB, or GPIOC.
- **CLK_ENABLE()**: Macro function that enables the clock for the specified peripheral, allowing it to receive power and function.

Simple Code Example

```
__HAL_RCC_GPIOA_CLK_ENABLE();  // Enables clock for GPIO port A
```

Code Example Explanation

- **Enables clock for GPIOA**: Powers up GPIO port A, making its pins ready for configuration and use.
- **Mandatory for GPIO operations**: This line is essential; without it, any configurations or functions involving GPIOA will fail.

Notes

- Enable clocks only for the GPIO ports in use to optimize power consumption.
- Each GPIO port (e.g., GPIOA, GPIOB) requires its own clock enable function.

Warnings

- Skipping clock enablement will result in ineffective GPIO configurations and operations on that port.

---

2. Configure GPIO Pin Mode

What is Configuring GPIO Pin Mode?

The GPIO pin mode setting determines how each GPIO pin behaves—whether it acts as an input, output, or alternate function pin.

Use Purpose

- **Define Pin Functionality**: Configures the pin to function as an input, output, or alternate function pin.
- **Control Signal Direction**: Sets the pin to either send (output) or receive (input) digital signals.

Syntax

```
GPIO_InitStruct.Mode = GPIO_MODE_xxx;
```

Syntax Explanation

- **GPIO_InitStruct**: A structure in the STM32 HAL library that holds the configuration settings for a GPIO pin.
- **.Mode**: A member of GPIO_InitStruct that defines the mode for the GPIO pin.
- **GPIO_MODE_xxx**: Mode options include:
  - **GPIO_MODE_INPUT**: Configures the pin to act as a digital input.
  - **GPIO_MODE_OUTPUT_PP**: Sets the pin as a push-pull output, where the pin actively drives high and low states.

- ○ **GPIO_MODE_AF_PP**: Configures the pin for an alternate function (e.g., UART, SPI) in push-pull mode.

Simple Code Example

```
GPIO_InitTypeDef GPIO_InitStruct;
GPIO_InitStruct.Pin = GPIO_PIN_5;
GPIO_InitStruct.Mode = GPIO_MODE_OUTPUT_PP;  // Sets pin as push-pull output
```

Code Example Explanation

- **Defines a configuration structure (GPIO_InitStruct)**: Holds settings for configuring GPIO.
- **Sets GPIO pin 5 as output**: Configures pin 5 to actively drive high and low voltages for controlling devices like LEDs.

Notes

- Push-pull mode is commonly used for digital outputs.
- For alternate functions (e.g., UART, SPI), use GPIO_MODE_AF_PP with the appropriate alternate function number.

Warnings

- Incorrect mode selection, such as configuring an input pin as an output, may result in hardware conflicts or malfunction.

3. Configure GPIO Speed
What is Configuring GPIO Speed?
The GPIO speed setting specifies how fast a GPIO pin can change states, affecting the maximum frequency of output signals. Faster speeds enable quick state changes but increase power consumption and noise.

Use Purpose

- **Control Signal Switching Rate**: Sets the maximum frequency at which a GPIO pin can switch between high and low.
- **Optimize Power and Performance**: Lower speeds conserve power, while higher speeds allow rapid changes for high-frequency signals.

Syntax

```
GPIO_InitStruct.Speed = GPIO_SPEED_xxx;
```

Syntax Explanation

- **GPIO_InitStruct**: Configuration structure for GPIO settings.
- **.Speed**: A member of `GPIO_InitStruct` that defines the switching speed of the GPIO pin.
- **GPIO_SPEED_xxx**: Options include:
  - **GPIO_SPEED_LOW**: Reduces power consumption, suitable for slower signals.
  - **GPIO_SPEED_MEDIUM**: Balances power usage and performance.
  - **GPIO_SPEED_HIGH**: Maximizes speed, suitable for high-frequency signals, but consumes more power.

Simple Code Example

```
GPIO_InitStruct.Speed = GPIO_SPEED_LOW;   // Configures the pin with low
speed
```

Code Example Explanation

- **Sets GPIO pin speed to low**: Reduces power usage, ideal for applications where the signal does not need to change rapidly.

Notes

- Choose lower speeds when possible to save power and reduce noise.
- Use higher speeds only when necessary for high-frequency signaling.

Warnings

- Using high-speed settings unnecessarily increases power consumption and can cause electromagnetic interference (EMI).

4. Set Output High

What is Setting Output High?

Setting a GPIO output high drives the pin to a logical high level, providing a positive voltage (typically 3.3V or 5V) to power or signal connected components.

Use Purpose

- **Activate External Devices**: Provides a high logic level to power LEDs, relays, or other components.
- **Signal Logical High**: Sets the pin to a logic "1" or high voltage level, commonly used to turn on connected components.

Syntax

```
HAL_GPIO_WritePin(GPIOx, GPIO_PIN_y, GPIO_PIN_SET);
```

Syntax Explanation

- **HAL_GPIO_WritePin**: HAL function that writes a logical state (high or low) to a specified GPIO pin.
- **GPIOx**: The GPIO port where the pin is located (e.g., `GPIOA`).
- **GPIO_PIN_y**: The specific GPIO pin number on the port (e.g., `GPIO_PIN_5`).
- **GPIO_PIN_SET**: Sets the output to a high logic level (3.3V or 5V, depending on system configuration).

Simple Code Example

```
HAL_GPIO_WritePin(GPIOA, GPIO_PIN_5, GPIO_PIN_SET);  // Sets PA5 to high
```

Code Example Explanation

- **Sets GPIO pin PA5 to high**: Provides a logic high voltage on PA5, turning on an LED or signaling a connected device.
- **Configures pin as output**: The pin must be set as an output in `GPIO_InitStruct` for this command to work.

Notes

- Ensure the pin is configured as an output before writing a high or low state.
- GPIO_PIN_SET drives the pin to a high voltage, turning on components like LEDs.

Warnings

- Writing high to an input-configured pin will have no effect and may cause conflicts in other configurations.

5. Set Output Low

What is Setting Output Low?

Setting a GPIO output low drives the pin to a logical low level, typically pulling it to 0V, effectively turning off or deactivating connected components.

Use Purpose

- **Deactivate External Devices**: Provides a low logic level to turn off LEDs, relays, or other components.
- **Signal Logical Low**: Sets the pin to a logic "0" or low voltage level.

Syntax

```
HAL_GPIO_WritePin(GPIOx, GPIO_PIN_y, GPIO_PIN_RESET);
```

Syntax Explanation

- **HAL_GPIO_WritePin**: HAL function that writes a logical state (high or low) to a specified GPIO pin.
- **GPIOx**: The GPIO port where the pin is located (e.g., GPIOA).
- **GPIO_PIN_y**: The specific GPIO pin number on the port (e.g., GPIO_PIN_5).
- **GPIO_PIN_RESET**: Sets the output to a low logic level (0V).

Simple Code Example

```
HAL_GPIO_WritePin(GPIOA, GPIO_PIN_5, GPIO_PIN_RESET);  // Sets PA5 to low
```

Code Example Explanation

- **Sets GPIO pin PA5 to low**: Provides a logic low voltage, turning off an LED or signaling a connected device to deactivate.

Notes

- Ensure the pin is configured as an output before setting a high or low state.
- GPIO_PIN_RESET pulls the pin voltage to ground (0V).

Warnings

- Writing low to an input-configured pin has no effect and may interfere with other configurations.

6. Toggle GPIO Pin

What is Toggling a GPIO Pin?

Toggling a GPIO pin switches it between high and low states. It is commonly used for blinking LEDs or generating square wave signals.

Use Purpose

- **Create Blinking or Pulsing Effects**: Toggling at regular intervals is useful for indicators.
- **Generate Square Waves**: Useful for producing clock or timing signals.

Syntax

```
HAL_GPIO_TogglePin(GPIOx, GPIO_PIN_y);
```

Syntax Explanation

- **HAL_GPIO_TogglePin**: HAL function that inverts the current state of the specified GPIO pin.
- **GPIOx**: The GPIO port where the pin is located (e.g., GPIOA).
- **GPIO_PIN_y**: The specific GPIO pin number to toggle on the port.

Simple Code Example

```
HAL_GPIO_TogglePin(GPIOA, GPIO_PIN_5);  // Toggles PA5
```

Code Example Explanation

- **Flips the state of GPIO pin PA5**: Changes PA5 from high to low or vice versa, creating a blinking effect when done repeatedly.

Notes

- Toggling in a timed loop can create blinking or pulsing effects.
- The toggle frequency affects visual effects, such as LED blinking rates.

Warnings

- Frequent toggling increases power consumption and may cause noise in high-frequency applications.

---

7. Read GPIO Input

What is Reading GPIO Input?

Reading GPIO input allows the STM32 to detect external signals, like button presses or sensor outputs, by checking the voltage level on the pin.

Use Purpose

- **Monitor External Devices**: Reads states from switches, buttons, or sensors.
- **Detect Digital Signals**: Checks if the input is high (3.3V) or low (0V).

Syntax

```
HAL_GPIO_ReadPin(GPIOx, GPIO_PIN_y);
```

Syntax Explanation

- **HAL_GPIO_ReadPin**: HAL function that reads the current digital state of a specified GPIO pin.
- **GPIOx**: The GPIO port (e.g., GPIOA).
- **GPIO_PIN_y**: The specific GPIO pin number on the port.
- **Returns**: GPIO_PIN_SET if the pin is high; GPIO_PIN_RESET if it is low.

Simple Code Example

```
if (HAL_GPIO_ReadPin(GPIOB, GPIO_PIN_0) == GPIO_PIN_SET) {
    // Perform an action if PB0 is high
}
```

Code Example Explanation

- **Reads GPIO pin PB0**: Checks if PB0 is at a high logic level.
- **Conditional logic**: Executes an action if PB0 is high, commonly used for detecting button presses.

Notes

- Use internal pull-up or pull-down resistors for stable input states.
- **GPIO_PIN_SET** and **GPIO_PIN_RESET** indicate high and low logic levels, respectively.

Warnings

- Floating input pins (without pull-up or pull-down) may produce unreliable readings.

Final Project: LED Toggle with Button Control

Project Objective

Create a circuit and code that toggles an LED on or off each time a button is pressed. This project demonstrates digital I/O by using GPIO pins for both input and output.

Project Circuit

Component	Pin Description	Connection Details
STM32 Microcontroller	GPIO PA5 (LED)	Configured as digital output
LED	Anode to PA5, Cathode to GND	Toggles state on button press
Button	GPIO PB0	Configured as digital input
Pull-down Resistor	PB0 to GND	Ensures stable default state

Circuit Analysis

- **GPIO PA5**: Configured as an output to control an LED.
- **GPIO PB0**: Configured as an input to detect button presses.
- **Button Press Logic**: Each press toggles the LED on or off.

Project Code

```c
#include "stm32f4xx_hal.h"
void GPIO_Config(void) {
    __HAL_RCC_GPIOA_CLK_ENABLE();  // Enable GPIOA clock
    __HAL_RCC_GPIOB_CLK_ENABLE();  // Enable GPIOB clock

    GPIO_InitTypeDef GPIO_InitStruct;
    // Configure LED Pin (PA5) as output
    GPIO_InitStruct.Pin = GPIO_PIN_5;
    GPIO_InitStruct.Mode = GPIO_MODE_OUTPUT_PP;
    GPIO_InitStruct.Pull = GPIO_NOPULL;
    GPIO_InitStruct.Speed = GPIO_SPEED_LOW;
    HAL_GPIO_Init(GPIOA, &GPIO_InitStruct);
    // Configure Button Pin (PB0) as input with pull-down
    GPIO_InitStruct.Pin = GPIO_PIN_0;
    GPIO_InitStruct.Mode = GPIO_MODE_INPUT;
    GPIO_InitStruct.Pull = GPIO_PULLDOWN;
    HAL_GPIO_Init(GPIOB, &GPIO_InitStruct);
}
int main(void) {
    HAL_Init();
    GPIO_Config();

    int button_state = 0;
    while (1) {
        if (HAL_GPIO_ReadPin(GPIOB, GPIO_PIN_0) == GPIO_PIN_SET) {
            HAL_Delay(100);  // Debounce delay
            if (button_state == 0) {
                HAL_GPIO_TogglePin(GPIOA, GPIO_PIN_5);  // Toggle LED
                button_state = 1;
            }
        } else {
            button_state = 0;
        }
    }
}
```

Save and Run

1. Save the code as main.c.
2. Compile and upload to the STM32 NUCLEO-F446RE using STM32CubeIDE or Keil.

Check Output

Expected behavior:

- The LED toggles on or off each time the button is pressed.

Analog I/O in STM32

Chapter Overview

Analog I/O allows STM32 microcontrollers to interact with real-world analog signals such as temperature or light intensity. The STM32 NUCLEO-F446RE board includes an Analog-to-Digital Converter (ADC) for reading analog inputs and a Digital-to-Analog Converter (DAC) for outputting analog voltages. This chapter covers the setup and operation of both the ADC and DAC and demonstrates a practical application.

Chapter Goal

- Understand how to configure the ADC to read analog signals.
- Learn how to use the DAC to generate adjustable analog output voltages.
- Complete a project to control an LED's brightness based on a potentiometer reading, demonstrating practical ADC and DAC usage.

Rules

- **Enable Clocks for ADC and DAC**: Ensure clocks are enabled for each peripheral to provide power.
- **Select ADC Channel**: Choose the correct ADC channel corresponding to the analog input pin.
- **Set ADC Resolution and Sampling Time**: Adjust these settings based on precision and speed requirements.
- **Choose DAC Output Channel**: Select the DAC output channel to control the analog output.
- **Use DMA for Continuous Sampling**: Consider using DMA (Direct Memory Access) for efficient, continuous ADC sampling if needed.

Syntax Table

Serial No	Topic	Code Snippet	Simple Example
1	Enable ADC Clock	`__HAL_RCC_ADCx_CLK_ENABLE()`	`__HAL_RCC_ADC1_CLK_ENABLE()`
2	Configure ADC Channel	`sConfig.Channel = ADC_CHANNEL_xx`	`sConfig.Channel = ADC_CHANNEL_0`
3	Start ADC Conversion	`HAL_ADC_Start(&hadc)`	`HAL_ADC_Start(&hadc1)`
4	Read ADC Value	`HAL_ADC_GetValue(&hadc)`	`adcValue = HAL_ADC_GetValue(&hadc1)`
5	Enable DAC Clock	`__HAL_RCC_DAC_CLK_ENABLE()`	`__HAL_RCC_DAC_CLK_ENABLE()`
6	Start DAC Output	`HAL_DAC_Start(&hdac, DAC_CHANNEL_x)`	`HAL_DAC_Start(&hdac, DAC_CHANNEL_1)`
7	Set DAC Output Value	`HAL_DAC_SetValue(&hdac, DAC_CHANNEL_x, DAC_ALIGN_12B_R, value)`	`HAL_DAC_SetValue(&hdac, DAC_CHANNEL_1, DAC_ALIGN_12B_R, 2048)`

Topic Explanations

1. Enable ADC Clock

What is Enabling the ADC Clock?

Enabling the ADC clock provides power to the ADC peripheral, allowing it to be configured and used for analog-to-digital conversion.

Use Purpose

- **Power the ADC Peripheral**: Activates the ADC clock, making it functional for reading analog signals.
- **Essential for ADC Configuration**: Without the clock, ADC configurations and operations will not work.

Syntax

```
__HAL_RCC_ADCx_CLK_ENABLE();
```

Syntax Explanation

- **__HAL_RCC**: Prefix indicating the function is part of Reset and Clock Control (RCC) in STM32's HAL library.
- **ADCx**: Specifies which ADC peripheral to enable, such as ADC1.
- **CLK_ENABLE()**: Macro to enable the clock, allowing the ADC peripheral to operate.

Simple Code Example

```
__HAL_RCC_ADC1_CLK_ENABLE();  // Enables clock for ADC1
```

Code Example Explanation

- **Enables ADC1 clock**: Provides power to ADC1, allowing it to be configured and used for analog-to-digital conversions.

Notes

- Each ADC peripheral requires its clock to be enabled individually.
- Without enabling the clock, any attempts to use ADC functions will fail.

Warnings

- Ensure only necessary ADC clocks are enabled to save power.

2. Configure ADC Channel

What is Configuring the ADC Channel?

The ADC channel selection determines which input pin the ADC will read from. Each ADC channel corresponds to a specific analog-capable pin.

Use Purpose

- **Select Analog Input**: Configures the correct ADC channel based on the input pin connected to the analog signal.

Syntax

```
sConfig.Channel = ADC_CHANNEL_xx;
```

Syntax Explanation

- **sConfig**: A structure that holds configuration settings for the ADC, including the channel and sampling time.
- **.Channel**: Member of the sConfig structure that specifies the ADC channel to sample.
- **ADC_CHANNEL_xx**: Specifies the ADC channel, such as ADC_CHANNEL_0, which corresponds to a specific pin.

Simple Code Example

```
ADC_ChannelConfTypeDef sConfig;
sConfig.Channel = ADC_CHANNEL_0;  // Configures the ADC to read from
channel 0
```

Code Example Explanation

- **Configures ADC to sample from channel 0**: Tells the ADC which pin to read from, with each channel mapped to a specific pin.

Notes

- Refer to the STM32 pinout for available ADC channels and their corresponding pins.
- Only analog-capable pins can be used as ADC channels.

Warnings

- Using a non-analog-capable pin as an ADC channel may cause errors or unexpected behavior.

3. Start ADC Conversion

What is Starting ADC Conversion?

Starting an ADC conversion initiates the process of reading the voltage on the configured pin and converting it into a digital value based on the ADC's resolution.

Use Purpose

- **Begin Analog Sampling**: Starts converting the analog signal to a digital value that can be used in the program.

Syntax

```
HAL_ADC_Start(&hadc);
```

Syntax Explanation

- **HAL_ADC_Start**: HAL function that starts the ADC conversion.
- **&hadc**: A pointer to the ADC handle, representing the ADC peripheral being used.

Simple Code Example

```
HAL_ADC_Start(&hadc1);  // Starts ADC1 conversion
```

Code Example Explanation

- **Initiates a conversion on ADC1**: Begins sampling the signal on the configured pin and converting it to a digital value.

Notes

- This function must be called each time a new conversion is needed unless continuous conversion mode is enabled.
- Ensure the ADC is configured before calling this function.

Warnings

- If the ADC conversion is not started, no digital value will be obtained from the input pin.

4. Read ADC Value

What is Reading ADC Value?

Reading the ADC value retrieves the result of the most recent conversion, providing a digital representation of the analog input signal.

Use Purpose

- **Obtain the Digital Value**: Retrieves the digital equivalent of the analog input voltage.

Syntax

```
HAL_ADC_GetValue(&hadc);
```

Syntax Explanation

- **HAL_ADC_GetValue**: HAL function that reads the most recent ADC conversion result.
- **&hadc**: Pointer to the ADC handle, which represents the specific ADC peripheral being used.

Simple Code Example

```
uint32_t adcValue;
adcValue = HAL_ADC_GetValue(&hadc1);  // Reads the converted value from
ADC1
```

Code Example Explanation

- **Stores ADC result in adcValue**: Reads the digital conversion result from ADC1, representing the voltage level on the input pin.

Notes

- The digital value range depends on the ADC resolution (e.g., 0 to 4095 for 12-bit).
- Higher ADC resolution provides more precision in measurements.

Warnings

- Ensure the ADC conversion is complete before reading to avoid incomplete results.

5. Enable DAC Clock

What is Enabling the DAC Clock?

Enabling the DAC clock powers the DAC peripheral, making it available for generating analog output signals.

Use Purpose

- **Activate DAC**: Powers the DAC peripheral, allowing it to output analog signals.

Syntax

```
__HAL_RCC_DAC_CLK_ENABLE();
```

Syntax Explanation

- **__HAL_RCC**: Prefix for Reset and Clock Control functions in STM32's HAL library.
- **DAC**: Specifies the Digital-to-Analog Converter (DAC) peripheral.
- **CLK_ENABLE()**: Macro that enables the clock for the DAC, making it functional.

Simple Code Example

```
__HAL_RCC_DAC_CLK_ENABLE();   // Enables DAC clock
```

Code Example Explanation

- **Enables DAC clock**: Allows the DAC to be used for analog signal generation by powering it.

Notes

- The DAC clock must be enabled before any DAC configurations or output operations.
- Disabling unused clocks can reduce power consumption.

Warnings

- If the DAC clock is not enabled, DAC functions will not operate.

6. Start DAC Output

What is Starting DAC Output?

Starting the DAC output initiates the conversion of digital values to analog voltages, generating a continuous analog output on the configured pin.

Use Purpose

- **Generate Analog Signals**: Begins outputting analog voltage based on the digital values provided.

Syntax

```
HAL_DAC_Start(&hdac, DAC_CHANNEL_x);
```

Syntax Explanation

- **HAL_DAC_Start**: HAL function that starts the DAC output.
- **&hdac**: Pointer to the DAC handle, representing the DAC peripheral.
- **DAC_CHANNEL_x**: Specifies the DAC channel, such as DAC_CHANNEL_1.

Simple Code Example

```
HAL_DAC_Start(&hdac, DAC_CHANNEL_1);  // Starts DAC output on channel 1
```

Code Example Explanation

- **Starts DAC output on channel 1**: Enables DAC channel 1 to output an analog voltage based on the set value.

Notes

- Only the enabled DAC channel will produce output.
- The DAC must be properly configured before starting the output.

Warnings

- Attempting to start DAC output without enabling the DAC clock will result in failure.

7. Set DAC Output Value

What is Setting DAC Output Value?

Setting the DAC output value determines the analog voltage level, providing control over the DAC's analog output.

Use Purpose

- **Adjust Analog Output**: Specifies the analog voltage level by setting a digital value for the DAC to convert.

Syntax

```
HAL_DAC_SetValue(&hdac, DAC_CHANNEL_x, DAC_ALIGN_12B_R, value);
```

Syntax Explanation

- **HAL_DAC_SetValue**: HAL function to set the DAC output.
- **&hdac**: Pointer to the DAC handle, representing the DAC peripheral.
- **DAC_CHANNEL_x**: Specifies the DAC channel (e.g., DAC_CHANNEL_1) to output from.
- **DAC_ALIGN_12B_R**: Specifies the 12-bit right-aligned data format for the output value.
- **value**: The digital value to be converted to an analog voltage (0 to 4095 for 12-bit resolution).

Simple Code Example

```
HAL_DAC_SetValue(&hdac, DAC_CHANNEL_1, DAC_ALIGN_12B_R, 2048);  // Sets
DAC to mid-scale output
```

Code Example Explanation

- **Sets DAC channel 1 to output mid-scale voltage**: A value of 2048 results in an output voltage of approximately 50% of the maximum range.

Notes

- The DAC value range depends on the resolution. For 12-bit alignment, values range from 0 to 4095.
- The analog output voltage scales based on the DAC reference voltage.

Warnings

- Setting values outside the valid range may cause unexpected DAC behavior.

Final Project: Potentiometer-Controlled LED Brightness

Project Objective

Use the ADC to read the position of a potentiometer and control an LED's brightness based on the potentiometer reading using the DAC.

Project Circuit

Component	Pin Description	Connection Details
STM32 Microcontroller	ADC Channel (Potentiometer)	Analog input connected to potentiometer
Potentiometer	VCC, GND, Analog Output	Connect output to ADC pin
LED	Anode to DAC, Cathode to GND	Adjust brightness using DAC output

Circuit Analysis

- **ADC Channel**: Reads voltage from the potentiometer to measure its position.
- **DAC Output**: Controls LED brightness based on the potentiometer reading.
- **Variable Brightness**: ADC readings adjust DAC output, allowing brightness changes.

Project Code

```c
#include "stm32f4xx_hal.h"

ADC_HandleTypeDef hadc1;
DAC_HandleTypeDef hdac;

void ADC_Config(void) {
    __HAL_RCC_ADC1_CLK_ENABLE();
    hadc1.Instance = ADC1;
    hadc1.Init.Resolution = ADC_RESOLUTION_12B;
```

```
    HAL_ADC_Init(&hadc1);
}

void DAC_Config(void) {
    __HAL_RCC_DAC_CLK_ENABLE();
    hdac.Instance = DAC;
    HAL_DAC_Init(&hdac);
    HAL_DAC_Start(&hdac, DAC_CHANNEL_1);
}

int main(void) {
    HAL_Init();
    ADC_Config();
    DAC_Config();

    while (1) {
        HAL_ADC_Start(&hadc1);
        if (HAL_ADC_PollForConversion(&hadc1, 100) == HAL_OK) {
            uint32_t adcValue = HAL_ADC_GetValue(&hadc1);
            HAL_DAC_SetValue(&hdac, DAC_CHANNEL_1, DAC_ALIGN_12B_R,
adcValue);
        }
        HAL_Delay(10);
    }
}
```

Save and Run

1. Save the code as `main.c`.
2. Compile and upload to the STM32 NUCLEO-F446RE using STM32CubeIDE or Keil.

Check Output

Expected behavior:

- The LED brightness changes based on potentiometer position.

Summary

This chapter covered ADC and DAC configurations on the STM32 NUCLEO-F446RE, demonstrating how to read and output analog signals. The final project showcased a potentiometer-controlled LED brightness application. These skills are foundational for interfacing with analog devices in embedded systems.

Advanced I/O in STM32

Chapter Overview

Advanced I/O capabilities extend the basic digital and analog I/O functionalities, allowing for more sophisticated control of external components. These include Pulse Width Modulation (PWM) for precise control of devices like motors and LEDs, interrupts for event-based handling, and I2C communication for interfacing with sensors and peripherals. This chapter covers configuring and using PWM, interrupts, and I2C on the STM32 NUCLEO-F446RE.

Chapter Goal

- Understand and configure PWM for applications like dimming LEDs or controlling motor speed.
- Learn how to use GPIO interrupts for event-driven applications.
- Configure I2C communication to interface with external I2C devices like sensors.
- Complete a project to control LED brightness using PWM and respond to button presses with interrupts.

Rules

- **Enable Clocks for Peripherals**: Ensure clocks are enabled for each peripheral (PWM timer, GPIO for interrupts, I2C).
- **Configure PWM Channels and Frequency**: Adjust PWM frequency and duty cycle based on the application requirements.
- **Set Up GPIO Interrupts**: Define GPIO pins as interrupt sources and configure NVIC for interrupt handling.
- **Initialize I2C Settings**: Set up I2C speed, address mode, and target device address for communication.
- **Use DMA for Continuous or High-Speed Operations**: When necessary, use DMA with PWM or I2C for efficient data handling.

Syntax Table

Serial No	Topic	Code Snippet	Simple Example
1	Enable PWM Timer Clock	`__HAL_RCC_TIMx_CLK_ENABLE()`	`__HAL_RCC_TIM3_CLK_ENABLE()`
2	Configure PWM Channel	`sConfigOC.Pulse = duty_cycle`	`sConfigOC.Pulse = 512`
3	Start PWM Output	`HAL_TIM_PWM_Start(&htim, TIM_CHANNEL_x)`	`HAL_TIM_PWM_Start(&htim3, TIM_CHANNEL_1)`
4	Enable GPIO Interrupt	`HAL_NVIC_EnableIRQ(EXTIx_IRQn)`	`HAL_NVIC_EnableIRQ(EXTI0_IRQn)`
5	Set Interrupt Priority	`HAL_NVIC_SetPriority(EXTIx_IRQn, priority)`	`HAL_NVIC_SetPriority(EXTI0_IRQn, 0)`
6	Enable I2C Clock	`__HAL_RCC_I2Cx_CLK_ENABLE()`	`__HAL_RCC_I2C1_CLK_ENABLE()`
7	Send I2C Data	`HAL_I2C_Master_Transmit(&hi2c, address, data, size, timeout)`	`HAL_I2C_Master_Transmit(&hi2c1, 0x50, data, 2, 100)`

Topic Explanations

1. Enable PWM Timer Clock

What is Enabling the PWM Timer Clock?

Enabling the PWM timer clock provides power to the timer peripheral, allowing it to be configured and used for PWM signal generation.

Use Purpose

- **Power Timer for PWM**: Activates the timer clock, allowing it to generate PWM signals on specific channels.
- **Essential for Timer Configuration**: Without enabling the clock, PWM settings and output will not function.

Syntax

```
__HAL_RCC_TIMx_CLK_ENABLE();
```

Syntax Explanation

- **__HAL_RCC**: Prefix used in STM32 HAL functions related to Reset and Clock Control (RCC).
- **TIMx**: Specifies the timer to enable, such as TIM1, TIM3, etc.
- **CLK_ENABLE()**: Macro function that enables the clock for the specified timer.

Simple Code Example

```
__HAL_RCC_TIM3_CLK_ENABLE();  // Enables clock for timer 3
```

Code Example Explanation

- **Enables the clock for TIM3**: Powers up the TIM3 peripheral, making it available for PWM or other timing-related functions.

Notes

- Each timer has a corresponding clock enable function.
- Choose the timer based on the available PWM channels.

Warnings

- Attempting to configure a timer without enabling its clock will result in a non-functional setup.

2. Configure PWM Channel

What is Configuring the PWM Channel?

The PWM channel setting defines the timer's behavior for generating a PWM signal, including the frequency and duty cycle.

Use Purpose

- **Generate Variable Signals**: Adjusts the signal's pulse width for applications like motor speed control or LED dimming.
- **Define PWM Characteristics**: Sets the timer's frequency and duty cycle to control output behavior.

Syntax

```
sConfigOC.Pulse = duty_cycle;
```

Syntax Explanation

- **sConfigOC**: A structure for the output compare settings of the timer used in PWM.
- **.Pulse**: A member of sConfigOC that sets the duty cycle, which defines the high time of the PWM signal.
- **duty_cycle**: A value representing the pulse width. Typically ranges from 0 to the timer's maximum count value, affecting the brightness or speed in applications.

Simple Code Example

```
TIM_OC_InitTypeDef sConfigOC;
sConfigOC.Pulse = 512;  // Sets a duty cycle of 50% for a 10-bit timer
```

Code Example Explanation

- **Sets duty cycle to 50%**: If the timer's maximum count is 1024, setting the pulse to 512 provides a 50% duty cycle, resulting in half the signal's period being high.

Notes

- A higher duty cycle means a longer high time within each period, increasing brightness or speed.
- Configure the timer's period and frequency before setting the duty cycle.

Warnings

- Setting the duty cycle beyond the timer's period may cause unexpected behavior.

3. Start PWM Output

What is Starting PWM Output?

Starting the PWM output initiates signal generation, creating a PWM waveform on the specified channel.

Use Purpose

- **Enable PWM Signal**: Begins outputting the PWM waveform on the selected pin.
- **Control Device Operation**: Used for precise control over devices like motors and LEDs.

Syntax

```
HAL_TIM_PWM_Start(&htim, TIM_CHANNEL_x);
```

Syntax Explanation

- **HAL_TIM_PWM_Start**: HAL function that starts the PWM output on a specified channel.
- **&htim**: Pointer to the timer handle that manages the timer configuration.
- **TIM_CHANNEL_x**: Specifies the timer channel (e.g., TIM_CHANNEL_1) to output the PWM signal.

Simple Code Example

```
HAL_TIM_PWM_Start(&htim3, TIM_CHANNEL_1);  // Starts PWM on TIM3
channel 1
```

Code Example Explanation

- **Begins PWM output on TIM3, channel 1**: Generates a PWM signal on the designated pin, typically connected to a motor or LED for control.

Notes

- Ensure the timer and channel are configured before starting the PWM output.
- Each timer has multiple channels that can generate independent PWM signals.

Warnings

- Ensure the timer's period, frequency, and duty cycle are set correctly before starting.

4. Enable GPIO Interrupt

What is Enabling a GPIO Interrupt?

Enabling a GPIO interrupt allows the microcontroller to detect external events, such as button presses, and respond to them immediately.

Use Purpose

- **Event-Driven Control**: Detects signals without needing to constantly poll, making the system more efficient.
- **Trigger External Events**: Useful for applications that require immediate response to inputs.

Syntax

```
HAL_NVIC_EnableIRQ(EXTIx_IRQn);
```

Syntax Explanation

- **HAL_NVIC_EnableIRQ**: HAL function that enables an interrupt request (IRQ) in the Nested Vectored Interrupt Controller (NVIC).
- **EXTIx_IRQn**: The interrupt line associated with the specific GPIO pin (e.g., EXTI0_IRQn for pin 0).

Simple Code Example

```
HAL_NVIC_EnableIRQ(EXTI0_IRQn);   // Enables interrupt on EXTI line 0
```

Code Example Explanation

- **Enables interrupt on EXTI line 0**: Allows the system to handle events on GPIO pin 0 immediately upon detection.

Notes

- Each GPIO pin can be configured to trigger an interrupt.
- Set up a callback function to specify what the interrupt should do when triggered.

Warnings

- Improper interrupt handling may lead to unexpected behavior or crashes.

5. Set Interrupt Priority

What is Setting Interrupt Priority?

Interrupt priority defines the importance of each interrupt. Lower priority values indicate higher importance, meaning higher priority interrupts will be serviced first.

Use Purpose

- **Manage System Responsiveness**: Ensures that critical interrupts are handled promptly.
- **Organize Multiple Interrupts**: Useful in systems with multiple interrupts where some are more time-sensitive.

Syntax

```
HAL_NVIC_SetPriority(EXTIx_IRQn, priority);
```

Syntax Explanation

- **HAL_NVIC_SetPriority**: HAL function that sets the priority of an interrupt.
- **EXTIx_IRQn**: The interrupt line associated with the GPIO pin.
- **priority**: Priority level (e.g., 0 for highest priority).

Simple Code Example

```
HAL_NVIC_SetPriority(EXTI0_IRQn, 0);  // Sets EXTI line 0 interrupt to
highest priority
```

Code Example Explanation

- **Assigns highest priority to EXTI line 0**: This interrupt will be handled before other lower-priority interrupts.

Notes

- Lower numerical values indicate higher priority.
- Use priorities wisely to ensure system stability.

Warnings

- Setting too many high-priority interrupts can impact system performance.

6. Enable I2C Clock

What is Enabling the I2C Clock?

Enabling the I2C clock provides power to the I2C peripheral, allowing it to be used for communication with external devices.

Use Purpose

- **Power I2C Peripheral**: Activates the clock for the I2C module to communicate with other I2C devices.
- **Enable I2C Operations**: Necessary to perform read and write operations over the I2C bus.

Syntax

```
__HAL_RCC_I2Cx_CLK_ENABLE();
```

Syntax Explanation

- **__HAL_RCC**: Prefix for Reset and Clock Control functions.
- **I2Cx**: Specifies the I2C peripheral to enable, such as I2C1 or I2C2.
- **CLK_ENABLE()**: Macro that enables the clock for the selected I2C module.

Simple Code Example

```
__HAL_RCC_I2C1_CLK_ENABLE();  // Enables clock for I2C1
```

Code Example Explanation

- **Enables clock for I2C1**: Powers the I2C1 peripheral to allow communication with connected I2C devices.

Notes

- Ensure the correct I2C clock is enabled based on the I2C peripheral in use.
- Each I2C module (e.g., I2C1, I2C2) requires individual clock enablement.

Warnings

- Using I2C functions without enabling the clock will cause errors.

7. Send I2C Data

What is Sending I2C Data?

Sending data over I2C allows the microcontroller to communicate with I2C-compatible devices such as sensors and EEPROMs.

Use Purpose

- **Transmit Data to I2C Devices**: Sends commands or data to devices on the I2C bus.
- **Interface with Sensors**: Used for applications like reading sensor data or controlling displays.

Syntax

```
HAL_I2C_Master_Transmit(&hi2c, address, data, size, timeout);
```

Syntax Explanation

- **HAL_I2C_Master_Transmit**: HAL function for sending data from the microcontroller to an I2C device.
- **&hi2c**: Pointer to the I2C handle, representing the I2C peripheral in use.
- **address**: The I2C address of the target device.
- **data**: Pointer to the data buffer to transmit.
- **size**: Number of bytes to transmit.
- **timeout**: Maximum wait time for data transmission to complete.

Simple Code Example

```
uint8_t data[2] = {0x01, 0x02};
HAL_I2C_Master_Transmit(&hi2c1, 0x50, data, 2, 100);  // Transmits 2
bytes to device at address 0x50
```

Code Example Explanation

- **Transmits two bytes to an I2C device at address 0x50**: Sends the contents of data to the I2C device.

Notes

- Set the target device's I2C address properly.
- Use appropriate data size and timeout based on the device's communication needs.

Warnings

- Mismatched addresses or data size errors can cause communication failure.

Final Project: LED PWM Control with Button Interrupt

Project Objective

Use PWM to control LED brightness and set up a button interrupt to toggle the LED between on and off states.

Project Circuit (In Table)

Component	Pin Description	Connection Details
STM32 Microcontroller	PWM Output (TIM3 Channel 1, PA6)	LED anode connected to PA6
Button	GPIO Interrupt (PB0)	Configured as interrupt input
Pull-down Resistor	PB0 to GND	Ensures stable button state

Circuit Analysis

- **PWM Output**: Controls LED brightness by adjusting duty cycle.
- **GPIO Interrupt (Button)**: Triggers LED on/off state change on each button press.

Project Code

```
#include "stm32f4xx_hal.h"

TIM_HandleTypeDef htim3;
int led_state = 0;

void PWM_Config(void) {
    __HAL_RCC_TIM3_CLK_ENABLE();
    htim3.Instance = TIM3;
    htim3.Init.Prescaler = 8399;
    htim3.Init.Period = 999;
    HAL_TIM_PWM_Init(&htim3);

    TIM_OC_InitTypeDef sConfigOC;
```

```
    sConfigOC.OCMode = TIM_OCMODE_PWM1;
    sConfigOC.Pulse = 500;  // 50% duty cycle
    HAL_TIM_PWM_ConfigChannel(&htim3, &sConfigOC, TIM_CHANNEL_1);
    HAL_TIM_PWM_Start(&htim3, TIM_CHANNEL_1);
}

void EXTI0_IRQHandler(void) {
    if (__HAL_GPIO_EXTI_GET_IT(GPIO_PIN_0) != RESET) {
        __HAL_GPIO_EXTI_CLEAR_IT(GPIO_PIN_0);
        HAL_GPIO_TogglePin(GPIOA, GPIO_PIN_6);
        led_state = !led_state;
    }
}
int main(void) {
    HAL_Init();
    PWM_Config();
    __HAL_RCC_GPIOA_CLK_ENABLE();
    __HAL_RCC_GPIOB_CLK_ENABLE();

    GPIO_InitTypeDef GPIO_InitStruct;
    GPIO_InitStruct.Pin = GPIO_PIN_0;
    GPIO_InitStruct.Mode = GPIO_MODE_IT_FALLING;
    GPIO_InitStruct.Pull = GPIO_PULLDOWN;
    HAL_GPIO_Init(GPIOB, &GPIO_InitStruct);
    HAL_NVIC_SetPriority(EXTI0_IRQn, 0);
    HAL_NVIC_EnableIRQ(EXTI0_IRQn);
    while (1) {
        // LED brightness is controlled by PWM, and on/off state by
button interrupt
    }
}
```

Save and Run

1. Save the code as main.c.
2. Compile and upload to the STM32 NUCLEO-F446RE using STM32CubeIDE or Keil.

Check Output

Expected behavior:

- The LED brightness is controlled by PWM.
- Pressing the button toggles the LED on or off.

Summary

This chapter covered PWM, GPIO interrupts, and I2C communication for advanced I/O operations on the STM32 NUCLEO-F446RE. The final project demonstrated PWM for LED brightness control and an interrupt to toggle the LED on/off with a button. These techniques enable versatile applications in embedded systems.

Timers in STM32

Chapter Overview

Timers are essential in embedded systems for managing delays, measuring time, and generating periodic signals. The STM32 NUCLEO-F446RE provides multiple hardware timers that can be configured for various timing functions, such as delays, pulse generation, and event timing. This chapter explains how to configure and use timers effectively, with a final project demonstrating LED blinking using timer-based interrupts.

Chapter Goal

- Understand how to configure and use timers for delay and periodic events.
- Learn how to create time delays and measure intervals.
- Learn how to use timer interrupts for event-driven applications.
- Complete a project using a timer to create a periodic LED blink.

Rules

- **Enable Timer Clock**: Enable the clock for each timer before configuring it.
- **Set Timer Prescaler and Period**: Adjust prescaler and period to define the timing interval.
- **Use Timer Interrupts for Event-Driven Applications**: Configure and enable interrupts for precise timing events.
- **Configure Timer for PWM**: Use timers to generate PWM signals if required.
- **Use Auto-Reload Register for Repeated Intervals**: Set the auto-reload register to repeat events automatically.

Syntax Table

Serial No	Topic	Code Snippet	Simple Example
1	Enable Timer Clock	`__HAL_RCC_TIMx_CLK_ENABLE()`	`__HAL_RCC_TIM2_CLK_ENABLE()`
2	Configure Timer Prescaler	`htim.Init.Prescaler = value`	`htim.Init.Prescaler = 8399`
3	Set Timer Period	`htim.Init.Period = value`	`htim.Init.Period = 999`
4	Start Timer	`HAL_TIM_Base_Start(&htim)`	`HAL_TIM_Base_Start(&htim2)`
5	Enable Timer Interrupt	`HAL_TIM_Base_Start_IT(&htim)`	`HAL_TIM_Base_Start_IT(&htim2)`
6	Set Timer Auto-Reload	`TIMx->ARR = value`	`TIM2->ARR = 1000`
7	Delay using HAL	`HAL_Delay(ms)`	`HAL_Delay(1000)`

Topic Explanations

1. Enable Timer Clock

What is Enabling the Timer Clock?

Enabling the timer clock powers the timer peripheral, allowing it to be configured and used for timing operations like delays, counters, or periodic signals.

Use Purpose

- **Power the Timer**: Activates the timer clock to make it functional.
- **Required for Timer Configuration**: Without enabling the clock, the timer settings will have no effect.

Syntax

```
__HAL_RCC_TIMx_CLK_ENABLE();
```

Syntax Explanation

- **__HAL_RCC**: Prefix for Reset and Clock Control functions in STM32's HAL library.
- **TIMx**: Specifies the timer to enable, such as TIM2, TIM3, etc.
- **CLK_ENABLE()**: Macro function that enables the clock, allowing the timer to operate.

Simple Code Example

```
__HAL_RCC_TIM2_CLK_ENABLE();  // Enables clock for timer 2
```

Code Example Explanation

- **Enables the clock for TIM2**: Powers up TIM2, making it available for timing functions like delay or periodic interrupts.

Notes

- Each timer requires a corresponding clock enable function.
- Refer to the STM32 datasheet to check available timers for the NUCLEO-F446RE.

Warnings

- Attempting to configure a timer without enabling its clock will lead to a non-functional setup.

---

2. Configure Timer Prescaler

What is Configuring the Timer Prescaler?

The prescaler divides the input clock frequency for the timer, controlling the timer's speed. Lower prescaler values make the timer faster, while higher values slow it down.

Use Purpose

- **Adjust Timer Speed**: Controls how fast the timer counts, allowing longer or shorter timing intervals.
- **Fine-Tune Timing**: Allows flexibility in setting the desired frequency or period for the timer.

Syntax

```
htim.Init.Prescaler = value;
```

Syntax Explanation

- **htim**: The timer handle that manages the timer configuration.
- **.Init.Prescaler**: A member of the `htim.Init` structure that defines the prescaler value.
- **value**: The prescaler value, which is a divisor applied to the timer's input clock.

Simple Code Example

```
htim2.Init.Prescaler = 8399;   // Sets the prescaler to 8399
```

Code Example Explanation

- **Divides the input clock by 8400** (prescaler + 1): Assuming a 84 MHz system clock, this results in a 10 kHz timer frequency.

Notes

- A higher prescaler value means a slower timer count.
- The prescaler must be set appropriately to achieve the desired timing interval.

Warnings

- Setting an incorrect prescaler value can cause timing errors.

---

3. Set Timer Period

What is Setting the Timer Period?

The timer period specifies the maximum count value before the timer resets or triggers an event. This is used to define the timing interval, such as how often an interrupt occurs.

Use Purpose

- **Define Timing Interval**: Sets the duration of the timer's counting cycle.
- **Trigger Events at Regular Intervals**: Useful for periodic tasks like blinking an LED.

Syntax

```
htim.Init.Period = value;
```

Syntax Explanation

- **htim**: The timer handle that manages the timer configuration.
- **.Init.Period**: A member of the `htim.Init` structure that defines the timer's counting period.
- **value**: The period value, representing the maximum count the timer reaches before it resets.

Simple Code Example

```
htim2.Init.Period = 999;  // Sets the period to 999
```

Code Example Explanation

- **Sets a 100 ms period**: If the timer frequency is 10 kHz, the timer resets every 100 ms (1000 counts).

Notes

- The period value depends on the prescaler and timer frequency.
- Setting the period correctly is essential for precise timing.

Warnings

- Incorrect period values may cause the timer to overflow too quickly or too slowly.

---

4. Start Timer

What is Starting the Timer?

Starting the timer initiates the counting process, allowing it to increment based on the configured frequency and period.

Use Purpose

- **Begin Timing Operation**: Starts the timer, enabling it to count and perform timing functions.
- **Enable Periodic Actions**: Used in applications that require continuous timing, like motor control.

Syntax

```
HAL_TIM_Base_Start(&htim);
```

Syntax Explanation

- **HAL_TIM_Base_Start**: HAL function that starts the basic timer operation.
- **&htim**: Pointer to the timer handle, which represents the timer being started.

Simple Code Example

```
HAL_TIM_Base_Start(&htim2);  // Starts TIM2
```

Code Example Explanation

- **Begins TIM2 operation**: TIM2 will now increment and perform any configured tasks, like triggering an interrupt.

Notes

- Ensure the timer is properly configured before starting it.
- Different timers may have additional configurations like output compare or PWM mode.

Warnings

- Starting the timer without configuration may lead to unintended operation.

---

5. Enable Timer Interrupt

What is Enabling Timer Interrupt?

Enabling a timer interrupt allows the timer to trigger an interrupt when it reaches a certain count, such as its period. This is useful for event-based applications that need regular timing.

Use Purpose

- **Event-Driven Timing**: Triggers an interrupt handler function periodically.
- **Precision Timing Tasks**: Used for precise timing applications, like motor control or sensor sampling.

Syntax

```
HAL_TIM_Base_Start_IT(&htim);
```

Syntax Explanation

- **HAL_TIM_Base_Start_IT**: HAL function that starts the timer with interrupts enabled.
- **&htim**: Pointer to the timer handle, representing the timer being started.

Simple Code Example

```
HAL_TIM_Base_Start_IT(&htim2);  // Starts TIM2 with interrupts enabled
```

Code Example Explanation

- **Enables TIM2 to trigger interrupts**: Each time TIM2 reaches its period, an interrupt is generated, calling a designated interrupt handler.

Notes

- Configure the interrupt handler function to define what the interrupt should do.
- Set the interrupt priority to manage timing conflicts.

Warnings

- Improper interrupt handling may cause timing errors or system crashes.

---

6. Set Timer Auto-Reload

What is Setting Timer Auto-Reload?

Auto-reload allows the timer to reset and continue counting automatically after reaching the period, creating a continuous cycle.

Use Purpose

- **Continuous Timer Operation**: Enables periodic interrupts without manual resetting.
- **Repeating Intervals**: Used in applications needing continuous timing, like PWM generation.

Syntax

```
TIMx->ARR = value;
```

Syntax Explanation

- **TIMx**: The specific timer register, such as TIM2 or TIM3.
- **ARR**: The auto-reload register, which defines the timer's reload value.
- **value**: The auto-reload value, which determines the timing interval.

Simple Code Example

```
TIM2->ARR = 1000;  // Sets auto-reload to 1000 for TIM2
```

Code Example Explanation

- **Sets TIM2 to auto-reload at 1000**: This causes the timer to reset and continue counting after reaching 1000.

Notes

- Setting ARR correctly is essential for periodic timing.
- Auto-reload is useful for PWM or periodic tasks.

Warnings

- Incorrect values in ARR can lead to timing inaccuracies.

---

7. Delay using HAL

What is Delay using HAL?

The HAL delay function creates a delay in milliseconds, pausing code execution for the specified time.

Use Purpose

- **Simple Time Delays**: Useful for debouncing or short pauses.
- **Non-Precise Timing**: Suitable for basic delays without strict timing requirements.

Syntax

```
HAL_Delay(ms);
```

Syntax Explanation

- **HAL_Delay**: HAL function that creates a blocking delay.
- **ms**: The delay duration in milliseconds.

Simple Code Example

```
HAL_Delay(1000);  // Delays execution for 1 second
```

Code Example Explanation

- **Pauses execution for 1000 ms**: Creates a 1-second delay, halting further code execution.

Notes

- HAL_Delay is not suitable for precise timing tasks.
- It blocks code execution, so avoid using it in time-sensitive sections.

Warnings

- Using long delays may affect system responsiveness.

Final Project: LED Blinking with Timer Interrupt

Project Objective

Use a timer interrupt to blink an LED at regular intervals without blocking code execution.

Project Circuit

Component	Pin Description	Connection Details
STM32 Microcontroller	Timer Output (TIM2)	Controls periodic LED blink
LED	Anode to GPIO Pin, Cathode to GND	LED toggles based on timer events

Circuit Analysis

- **TIM2**: Configured to generate periodic interrupts.
- **LED Toggle**: The LED toggles state each time the interrupt occurs, creating a blinking effect.

Project Code

```
#include "stm32f4xx_hal.h"

TIM_HandleTypeDef htim2;
void Timer_Config(void) {
    __HAL_RCC_TIM2_CLK_ENABLE();
    htim2.Instance = TIM2;
    htim2.Init.Prescaler = 8399;
    htim2.Init.Period = 9999;  // 1-second interval with 10 kHz timer
frequency
    HAL_TIM_Base_Init(&htim2);
    HAL_TIM_Base_Start_IT(&htim2);
}
void TIM2_IRQHandler(void) {
    if (__HAL_TIM_GET_FLAG(&htim2, TIM_FLAG_UPDATE) != RESET) {
        __HAL_TIM_CLEAR_IT(&htim2, TIM_IT_UPDATE);
        HAL_GPIO_TogglePin(GPIOA, GPIO_PIN_5);  // Toggles LED on PA5
    }
}
int main(void) {
    HAL_Init();
    __HAL_RCC_GPIOA_CLK_ENABLE();

    GPIO_InitTypeDef GPIO_InitStruct;
    GPIO_InitStruct.Pin = GPIO_PIN_5;
    GPIO_InitStruct.Mode = GPIO_MODE_OUTPUT_PP;
    GPIO_InitStruct.Pull = GPIO_NOPULL;
    GPIO_InitStruct.Speed = GPIO_SPEED_LOW;
    HAL_GPIO_Init(GPIOA, &GPIO_InitStruct);

    Timer_Config();
    while (1) {
        // LED blink controlled by TIM2 interrupt
    }
}
```

Save and Run

1. Save the code as `main.c`.
2. Compile and upload to the STM32 NUCLEO-F446RE using STM32CubeIDE or Keil.

Check Output

Expected behavior:

- The LED connected to PA5 blinks every second based on the TIM2 interrupt.

Constants and Variables in STM32

Chapter Overview

Constants and variables are foundational in embedded systems programming, allowing you to store and manipulate data. Constants hold fixed values that do not change, while variables can store information that changes over time. Understanding how to declare, use, and manage constants and variables effectively is crucial in STM32 embedded applications.

Chapter Goal

- Learn how to declare, initialize, and use constants and variables in C.
- Understand the different types of variables (local, global, static) and their scope.
- Explore best practices for using constants and variables in embedded systems programming.

Rules

- **Use Constants for Fixed Values**: Store values that should remain the same throughout the program using constants.
- **Declare Variables Based on Scope Needs**: Use local variables for temporary data, global variables for shared data, and static variables to retain values across function calls.
- **Choose the Correct Data Type**: Optimize memory and processing by selecting the appropriate data type for each variable.
- **Avoid Unnecessary Global Variables**: Limit the use of global variables to reduce memory usage and prevent data conflicts.

Syntax Table

Serial No	Topic	Code Snippet	Simple Example
1	Declare Constant	`#define CONSTANT_NAME value`	`#define PI 3.14159`
2	Declare Global Variable	`data_type variable_name;`	`int counter;`
3	Declare Local Variable	`data_type variable_name;`	`float temperature;`
4	Initialize Variable	`data_type variable_name = value;`	`int count = 0;`
5	Declare Static Variable	`static data_type variable_name = value;`	`static int persistent_value = 5;`
6	Declare Constant with const	`const data_type variable_name = value;`	`const float GRAVITY = 9.81;`
7	Scope of Variables	Local: Within function, Global: Outside functions	`void func() { int x = 5; }` `int y = 10;`

Topic Explanations

1. Declare Constant

What is Declaring a Constant?

Declaring a constant allows you to define a fixed value that remains unchanged throughout the program. In embedded systems, constants are often used for settings, configuration values, or mathematical constants.

Use Purpose

- **Store Fixed Values**: Holds values that should not change during program execution, such as PI, speed limits, or sensor thresholds.
- **Improve Code Readability**: Named constants provide a clear description of their purpose, improving code readability.

Syntax

```
#define CONSTANT_NAME value
```

Syntax Explanation

- **#define**: Preprocessor directive used to create constants.
- **CONSTANT_NAME**: The name of the constant, typically written in uppercase to distinguish it from variables.
- **value**: The fixed value assigned to the constant.

Simple Code Example

```
#define PI 3.14159   // Declares a constant for the value of PI
```

Code Example Explanation

- **Defines PI as 3.14159**: PI is a constant and cannot be modified, representing the mathematical constant π.

Notes

- Constants declared with #define do not take up memory space.
- Use uppercase names for constants to distinguish them from variables.

Warnings

- Do not attempt to change a constant's value, as it may lead to unexpected behavior.

2. Declare Global Variable

What is Declaring a Global Variable?

A global variable is accessible from any part of the program. Declaring a variable globally allows it to be shared across multiple functions.

Use Purpose

- **Share Data Across Functions**: Useful for counters, flags, and configuration values that need to be accessed globally.
- **Store Persistent Data**: Retains value throughout the program's execution.

Syntax

```
data_type variable_name;
```

Syntax Explanation

- **data_type**: Specifies the type of the variable, such as int, float, or char.
- **variable_name**: The name of the variable, which follows naming rules and conventions.

Simple Code Example

```
int counter;  // Declares a global integer variable named 'counter'
```

Code Example Explanation

- **Defines counter as a global integer**: counter can be accessed and modified from any function within the program.

Notes

- Global variables are generally declared at the top of the program file.
- Use descriptive names to indicate the purpose of global variables.

Warnings

- Excessive use of global variables can lead to memory conflicts and make debugging more difficult.

3. Declare Local Variable

What is Declaring a Local Variable?

A local variable is declared within a function and is accessible only within that function. Local variables help encapsulate data within specific parts of a program.

Use Purpose

- **Limit Variable Scope**: Local variables are confined to the function they are declared in, preventing unintended modifications from other parts of the program.
- **Manage Temporary Data**: Useful for storing temporary data needed only within a specific function.

Syntax

```
data_type variable_name;
```

Syntax Explanation

- **data_type**: Defines the type of the variable, such as `int`, `float`, or `char`.
- **variable_name**: The name of the variable, following naming conventions.

Simple Code Example

```
void exampleFunction() {
    int temperature = 25;  // Declares a local variable 'temperature'
}
```

Code Example Explanation

- **Defines `temperature` as a local integer**: `temperature` is confined to `exampleFunction` and cannot be accessed outside it.

Notes

- Local variables are initialized each time the function is called.
- Use meaningful names to represent the data stored in local variables.

Warnings

- Local variables do not retain their values between function calls.

4. Initialize Variable

What is Initializing a Variable?

Initializing a variable involves assigning it an initial value at the time of declaration. This ensures the variable has a defined value before it is used.

Use Purpose

- **Avoid Uninitialized Data**: Initialization prevents the use of undefined or random values.
- **Prepare Variables for Use**: Sets starting values for counters, flags, or configuration parameters.

Syntax

```
data_type variable_name = value;
```

Syntax Explanation

- **data_type**: Specifies the type of the variable.
- **variable_name**: The name of the variable.
- **value**: The initial value assigned to the variable.

Simple Code Example

```
int count = 0;  // Initializes 'count' with a value of 0
```

Code Example Explanation

- **Sets count to 0**: Ensures count starts with a defined value, avoiding errors from uninitialized data.

Notes

- Always initialize variables before using them in calculations or logic.
- For larger arrays, consider initializing values in loops.

Warnings

- Using uninitialized variables may produce unpredictable results.

5. Declare Static Variable

What is Declaring a Static Variable?

A static variable retains its value between function calls, even if it is declared locally within a function. Static variables are useful for maintaining state across multiple function executions.

Use Purpose

- **Maintain State**: Stores values that need to persist across function calls, like counters or configuration flags.
- **Limit Scope but Retain Value**: Static variables are local to the function but keep their value between calls.

Syntax

```
static data_type variable_name = value;
```

Syntax Explanation

- **static**: The keyword that makes the variable retain its value across function calls.
- **data_type**: Specifies the type of the variable.
- **variable_name**: The name of the variable.
- **value**: Initial value assigned to the variable.

Simple Code Example

```
void countCalls() {
    static int callCount = 0;   // Static variable to count function calls
    callCount++;
}
```

Code Example Explanation

- **Increments `callCount` each time `countCalls` is called**: Since `callCount` is static, it retains its value between calls, making it useful for tracking the number of times the function runs.

Notes

- Static variables are initialized only once and retain their value throughout program execution.
- Useful for counters or flags within functions.

Warnings

- Overuse of static variables can increase memory usage.

6. Declare Constant with `const`

What is Declaring a Constant with `const`?

The `const` keyword is another way to define constants, making a variable's value unchangeable after it is initialized. Unlike #define, `const` constants have a type and are stored in memory.

Use Purpose

- **Store Unmodifiable Values**: Holds values that should remain constant throughout the program.
- **Increase Code Readability**: Using `const` gives the compiler additional information about the variable's intent.

Syntax

```
const data_type variable_name = value;
```

Syntax Explanation

- **const**: Keyword indicating that the variable's value cannot be modified.
- **data_type**: Specifies the type of the variable.
- **variable_name**: The name of the constant.
- **value**: The constant's initial value.

Simple Code Example

```
const float GRAVITY = 9.81;   // Declares a constant for gravity
```

Code Example Explanation

- **Defines GRAVITY as a constant float with a value of 9.81**: This value cannot be modified, ensuring GRAVITY remains consistent.

Notes

- Use `const` for fixed values with a defined type, unlike #define which is a preprocessor directive.
- Constants declared with `const` are stored in memory.

Warnings

- Attempting to change a `const` variable will result in a compilation error.

7. Scope of Variables

What is Variable Scope?

Variable scope determines where a variable can be accessed in the program. Variables can be local (only within a function) or global (accessible throughout the program).

Use Purpose

- **Manage Data Accessibility**: Control where variables can be accessed and modified to avoid conflicts and errors.
- **Organize Program Structure**: Use local variables for temporary data and global variables for shared data.

Syntax

```
// Local variable
void func() {
    int x = 5;  // Local to func
}

// Global variable
int y = 10;  // Accessible from any function
```

Syntax Explanation

- **Local variables**: Declared within functions and are only accessible in that function.
- **Global variables**: Declared outside of functions and accessible from any part of the program.

Simple Code Example

```
void increment() {
    int count = 0;  // Local variable
    count++;
}

int total = 0;  // Global variable
```

Code Example Explanation

- **count is a local variable**: Exists only within `increment`.
- **total is a global variable**: Accessible from any function in the program.

Notes

- Limit global variables to prevent unexpected data changes.
- Local variables are ideal for temporary data that doesn't need to persist.

Warnings

- Overuse of global variables can lead to data conflicts.

Final Project: Using Constants and Variables to Control an LED

Project Objective

Create a program to blink an LED at a specific interval using constants and variables.

Project Circuit (In Table)

Component	Pin Description	Connection Details
STM32 Microcontroller	GPIO Output (PA5)	Controls LED blinking
LED	Anode to PA5, Cathode to GND	LED toggles based on interval

Circuit Analysis

- **GPIO PA5**: Configured to control LED blinking.
- **Interval Control**: The interval for blinking is defined by a constant.

Project Code

```
#include "stm32f4xx_hal.h"

#define LED_PIN GPIO_PIN_5   // Constant for LED pin
#define BLINK_DELAY 1000     // Constant for delay interval in
milliseconds

void LED_Init(void) {
    __HAL_RCC_GPIOA_CLK_ENABLE();
    GPIO_InitTypeDef GPIO_InitStruct = {0};
    GPIO_InitStruct.Pin = LED_PIN;
    GPIO_InitStruct.Mode = GPIO_MODE_OUTPUT_PP;
    GPIO_InitStruct.Pull = GPIO_NOPULL;
    GPIO_InitStruct.Speed = GPIO_SPEED_LOW;
    HAL_GPIO_Init(GPIOA, &GPIO_InitStruct);
}

int main(void) {
    HAL_Init();
    LED_Init();

    while (1) {
        HAL_GPIO_TogglePin(GPIOA, LED_PIN);  // Toggle LED state
        HAL_Delay(BLINK_DELAY);                    // Delay using constant
interval
    }
}
```

Save and Run

1. Save the code as `main.c`.
2. Compile and upload to the STM32 NUCLEO-F446RE using STM32CubeIDE or Keil.

Check Output

Expected behavior:

- The LED connected to PA5 blinks at a 1-second interval based on the BLINK_DELAY constant.

Summary

This chapter covered the use of constants and variables, including types, scope, and initialization. The final project demonstrated how to control LED blinking using constants for configuration and variables for data storage, providing a practical foundation in STM32 programming.

Data Types in STM32

Chapter Overview

Data types are fundamental in C programming, especially in embedded systems, where efficient memory usage and precise data representation are crucial. The STM32 NUCLEO-F446RE uses C data types to represent various forms of data, such as integers, floating-point numbers, characters, and pointers. Understanding and choosing the appropriate data type helps optimize memory usage and processing efficiency, which is essential in embedded systems programming.

Chapter Goal

- Understand the basic data types available in C, such as integers, floating-point numbers, characters, and pointers.
- Learn how to choose the correct data type based on memory, precision, and range requirements.
- Explore typedefs and custom data types for improved code readability and modularity.

Rules

- **Use Integer Types for Whole Numbers**: Choose signed or unsigned integer types based on the application requirements.
- **Choose Floating-Point Types for Precise Calculations**: Use floating-point types for calculations that require decimal precision.
- **Use Characters for ASCII Text**: Use the char type to represent single ASCII characters.
- **Apply Typedefs for Custom Types**: Use typedef to create custom names for data types, improving code readability.
- **Optimize Data Type Size**: Select the smallest data type necessary to minimize memory usage and processing load.

Syntax Table

Serial No	Topic	Code Snippet	Simple Example
1	Integer Types	`int variable_name;`	`int counter;`
2	Unsigned Integer	`unsigned int variable_name;`	`unsigned int age;`
3	Short Integer	`short int variable_name;`	`short int temperature;`
4	Long Integer	`long int variable_name;`	`long int distance;`
5	Floating-Point Types	`float variable_name;`	`float height;`
6	Character Type	`char variable_name;`	`char letter;`
7	Define Typedef	`typedef existing_type new_name;`	`typedef unsigned int uint;`

Topic Explanations

1. Integer Types

What are Integer Types?

Integer types represent whole numbers, both positive and negative. They are commonly used in embedded systems for counters, indexes, and flags where fractional values are not required.

Use Purpose

- **Store Whole Numbers**: Holds integers without decimal places, such as counters, flags, or states.
- **Optimize Memory for Whole Numbers**: Uses minimal memory for representing whole numbers.

Syntax

```
int variable_name;
```

Syntax Explanation

- **int**: Specifies the data type as an integer, typically 4 bytes (32 bits) on STM32 microcontrollers.
- **variable_name**: The name of the integer variable, following naming conventions.

Simple Code Example

```
int counter = 10;   // Declares an integer variable with an initial
value of 10
```

Code Example Explanation

- **Defines counter as an integer with a value of 10**: This integer variable can store whole numbers and is used for counting.

Notes

- Integer size on STM32 is typically 4 bytes, allowing values from approximately -2 billion to +2 billion.
- Negative values are stored using two's complement representation.

Warnings

- Integer overflow can occur if the value exceeds the maximum range for the data type.

2. Unsigned Integer

What is an Unsigned Integer?

An unsigned integer can only represent non-negative numbers, doubling the range of positive values compared to a signed integer. This is useful for quantities that cannot be negative, like age or count.

Use Purpose

- **Store Non-Negative Values**: Suitable for values that are always positive, such as counts or IDs.
- **Increase Range**: Offers a larger positive range than signed integers.

Syntax

```
unsigned int variable_name;
```

Syntax Explanation

- **unsigned**: Modifier that removes the sign bit, allowing only non-negative values.
- **int**: Specifies the integer data type.
- **variable_name**: The name of the variable, following standard naming rules.

Simple Code Example

```
unsigned int age = 25;  // Declares an unsigned integer with a value of 25
```

Code Example Explanation

- **Defines age as an unsigned integer with a value of 25**: Since it's unsigned, age cannot hold negative values.

Notes

- Unsigned integers have a range from 0 to approximately 4 billion.
- Use unsigned integers where negative values are irrelevant.

Warnings

- Using negative values with unsigned variables can lead to unexpected behavior.

3. Short Integer

What is a Short Integer?

A short integer is a smaller integer type, typically 2 bytes (16 bits), that consumes less memory. It's ideal for small-range values like sensor readings or flags.

Use Purpose

- **Conserve Memory**: Uses less memory than a standard integer.
- **Store Small-Range Values**: Suitable for variables with a smaller range.

Syntax

```
short int variable_name;
```

Syntax Explanation

- **short**: Specifies a smaller integer type.
- **int**: Specifies the integer data type.
- **variable_name**: The name of the variable.

Simple Code Example

```
short int temperature = -10;   // Declares a short integer with a value
of -10
```

Code Example Explanation

- **Defines temperature as a short integer**: Uses 2 bytes to store values, conserving memory for applications with limited memory space.

Notes

- Range is approximately -32,768 to +32,767 for a signed short integer.
- Commonly used in embedded systems where memory is limited.

Warnings

- Be cautious of overflow when using short integers for calculations.

4. Long Integer

What is a Long Integer?

A long integer is an extended integer type, typically 4 bytes (32 bits) or more, that provides a larger range. It is useful for large counts or values.

Use Purpose

- **Store Large Numbers**: Suitable for applications requiring a larger range of integer values.
- **Retain Precision**: Useful when small data types may overflow.

Syntax

```
long int variable_name;
```

Syntax Explanation

- **long**: Specifies an extended integer type.
- **int**: Specifies the integer data type.
- **variable_name**: The name of the variable.

Simple Code Example

```
long int distance = 123456;   // Declares a long integer with a value of 123456
```

Code Example Explanation

- **Defines distance as a long integer with a value of 123456**: Suitable for values beyond the standard integer range.

Notes

- Long integers are generally 4 bytes, providing a wider range of values.
- Commonly used for large counts, distances, or similar measurements.

Warnings

- Use only when necessary, as long integers require more memory.

5. Floating-Point Types

What are Floating-Point Types?

Floating-point types represent numbers with decimal points, used in calculations requiring precision. The two main types are `float` and `double`.

Use Purpose

- **Perform Decimal Calculations**: Ideal for applications involving fractions or precise measurements.
- **Retain Precision in Calculations**: Provides fractional accuracy.

Syntax

```
float variable_name;
```

Syntax Explanation

- **float**: Specifies a floating-point data type.
- **variable_name**: The name of the floating-point variable.

Simple Code Example

```
float height = 5.75;  // Declares a floating-point variable with a
value of 5.75
```

Code Example Explanation

- **Defines `height` as a float with a value of 5.75**: Suitable for representing real numbers with fractional parts.

Notes

- `float` is typically 4 bytes and provides around 6-7 decimal digits of precision.
- `double` is often 8 bytes, offering greater precision and range.

Warnings

- Floating-point calculations can be slower than integer operations in embedded systems.

6. Character Type

What is the Character Type?

The char type represents a single ASCII character and typically occupies 1 byte. It is useful for text data or representing small integer values.

Use Purpose

- **Store Characters**: Holds single characters, such as letters or symbols.
- **Represent Small Integers**: Can be used to store small integer values (0 to 255 for unsigned char).

Syntax

```
char variable_name;
```

Syntax Explanation

- **char**: Specifies the character data type.
- **variable_name**: The name of the character variable.

Simple Code Example

```
char letter = 'A';  // Declares a character variable with the value 'A'
```

Code Example Explanation

- **Defines letter as a character with the value 'A'**: Useful for storing single ASCII characters.

Notes

- char can be signed or unsigned, depending on the application.
- Use char arrays to represent strings.

Warnings

- Characters can only store one ASCII symbol or small integers.

7. Define Typedef

What is Typedef?

`typedef` creates an alias for an existing data type, improving code readability and modularity. It is commonly used to define custom data types.

Use Purpose

- **Simplify Data Types**: Provides a shorter or more descriptive name for complex data types.
- **Enhance Code Readability**: Useful for creating names that represent the variable's purpose.

Syntax

```
typedef existing_type new_name;
```

Syntax Explanation

- **typedef**: Keyword that defines a new name for an existing type.
- **existing_type**: The original data type.
- **new_name**: The alias or custom name for the data type.

Simple Code Example

```
typedef unsigned int uint;  // Defines 'uint' as an alias for 'unsigned int'
```

Code Example Explanation

- **Creates uint as an alias for unsigned int**: Simplifies code by using `uint` in place of `unsigned int`.

Notes

- Use `typedef` for complex types like structs or pointer types to improve readability.
- Commonly used in embedded systems to define custom types for specific applications.

Warnings

- Avoid creating confusing or redundant typedefs that may complicate the code.

Final Project: Using Different Data Types to Control an LED Pattern

Project Objective

Create a program to control an LED pattern based on an integer counter and control delay with floating-point calculations.

Project Circuit

Component	Pin Description	Connection Details
STM32 Microcontroller	GPIO Output (PA5)	Controls LED pattern
LED	Anode to PA5, Cathode to GND	LED blinks based on counter and delay

Circuit Analysis

- **GPIO PA5**: Configured as the output pin to control LED.
- **Data Types for Control**: Integer for counter, float for delay calculation.

Project Code

```
#include "stm32f4xx_hal.h"

#define LED_PIN GPIO_PIN_5

void LED_Init(void) {
    __HAL_RCC_GPIOA_CLK_ENABLE();
    GPIO_InitTypeDef GPIO_InitStruct = {0};
    GPIO_InitStruct.Pin = LED_PIN;
    GPIO_InitStruct.Mode = GPIO_MODE_OUTPUT_PP;
    GPIO_InitStruct.Pull = GPIO_NOPULL;
    GPIO_InitStruct.Speed = GPIO_SPEED_LOW;
    HAL_GPIO_Init(GPIOA, &GPIO_InitStruct);
}

int main(void) {
    HAL_Init();
    LED_Init();
```

```
int counter = 0;
float delay = 500.0;  // Initial delay in milliseconds

while (1) {
    HAL_GPIO_TogglePin(GPIOA, LED_PIN);
    counter++;                      // Increment counter
    delay = 500.0 / (1 + counter % 5);  // Adjust delay based on
counter
    HAL_Delay((int)delay);          // Apply delay
}
}
```

Save and Run

1. Save the code as `main.c`.
2. Compile and upload to the STM32 NUCLEO-F446RE using STM32CubeIDE or Keil.

Check Output

Expected behavior:

- The LED connected to PA5 blinks with an increasing frequency as the counter increments, using different data types for control.

Summary

This chapter covered essential data types in C for STM32 programming, including integers, floating-point numbers, characters, and typedefs. The final project demonstrated data type applications in LED control, showing how different types can be used effectively in embedded systems. Understanding data types and their correct usage is fundamental for efficient and optimized embedded programming.

Data Conversion in STM32

Chapter Overview

Data conversion allows the transformation of one data type to another, such as converting integers to floating-point numbers or strings to numbers. Conversions are essential in embedded systems to ensure that data is handled correctly, especially when interfacing with sensors, displays, or external devices. This chapter covers different types of conversions, including implicit and explicit conversions, along with techniques specific to embedded systems.

Chapter Goal

- Understand the difference between implicit and explicit type conversions in C.
- Learn to convert between integer and floating-point types.
- Explore techniques for converting numbers to strings and vice versa.
- Apply data conversion techniques in a practical project for displaying sensor data.

Rules

- **Use Implicit Conversions with Caution**: Implicit conversions can lead to data loss, especially when converting from a larger to a smaller data type.
- **Prefer Explicit Conversions for Clarity**: Use explicit type casting to ensure the intended conversion, avoiding unexpected results.
- **Avoid Precision Loss**: When converting from float to int, consider rounding if necessary to minimize data loss.
- **Use Standard Library Functions for String Conversions**: Utilize functions like sprintf, atoi, and atof for converting between strings and numbers.
- **Check for Conversion Errors**: Handle errors, especially in string conversions, to avoid unexpected behavior.

Syntax Table

Serial No	Topic	Code Snippet	Simple Example
1	Implicit Conversion	`result = integer + float;`	`int i = 5; float f = 2.5; float result = i + f;`
2	Explicit Conversion (Casting)	`(new_type)variable_name`	`float f = 3.14; int i = (int)f;`
3	Integer to Float Conversion	`float_var = (float)int_var;`	`int i = 10; float f = (float)i;`
4	Float to Integer Conversion	`int_var = (int)float_var;`	`float f = 2.7; int i = (int)f;`
5	String to Integer Conversion	`int_var = atoi(string_var);`	`char s[] = "123"; int i = atoi(s);`
6	String to Float Conversion	`float_var = atof(string_var);`	`char s[] = "3.14"; float f = atof(s);`
7	Integer to String Conversion	`sprintf(string_var, "%d", int_var);`	`int i = 100; char s[10]; sprintf(s, "%d", i);`

8	Float to String Conversion	`sprintf(string_var, "%.2f", float_var);`	`float f = 3.14; char s[10]; sprintf(s, "%.2f", f);`

Topic Explanations

1. Implicit Conversion

What is Implicit Conversion?

Implicit conversion happens automatically when one data type is assigned to a variable of another compatible type. In C, this occurs when an expression combines different types, and the compiler converts one type to another without explicit instructions.

Use Purpose

- **Automatic Conversion in Expressions**: Simplifies code by automatically adjusting types in mixed-type expressions.
- **Maintain Precision in Calculations**: When combining integers and floats, implicit conversion promotes the integer to float for accurate results.

Syntax

```
result = integer + float;
```

Syntax Explanation

- **integer**: An integer variable or value.
- **+ float**: The integer is implicitly converted to a float to perform the addition with the float value.
- **result**: The result is stored as a float, maintaining precision.

Simple Code Example

```
int i = 5;
float f = 2.5;
float result = i + f;   // i is implicitly converted to float
```

Code Example Explanation

- **Integer i is implicitly converted to float**: The addition produces a floating-point result of 7.5, stored in `result`.

Notes
- Implicit conversion occurs when combining types, such as adding an integer to a float.
- Conversion follows a hierarchy: smaller types are converted to larger types.

Warnings
- Implicit conversions can cause data loss when converting from float to int.

---

2. Explicit Conversion (Casting)

What is Explicit Conversion (Casting)?

Explicit conversion, or casting, allows you to convert a variable to a specific type manually. This provides more control over data conversions and avoids unintended implicit conversions.

Use Purpose
- **Ensure Correct Type Conversion**: Useful when converting between incompatible types.
- **Avoid Data Loss Warnings**: Explicit conversion prevents compiler warnings about possible data loss.

Syntax

```
(new_type)variable_name;
```

Syntax Explanation
- **(new_type)**: The type to which you want to convert the variable.
- **variable_name**: The variable to convert.

Simple Code Example

```
float f = 3.14;
int i = (int)f;  // Explicitly converts f to int, resulting in 3
```

Code Example Explanation

- **Converts f to an integer**: By casting, f is truncated to 3, as the decimal part is removed.

Notes
- Explicit conversion is necessary when converting from `float` to `int` or between incompatible types.
- Casting is also used to avoid unintended implicit conversions.

Warnings
- Casting a floating-point number to an integer discards the fractional part.

---

3. Integer to Float Conversion

What is Integer to Float Conversion?
Integer-to-float conversion is an explicit type conversion that changes an integer to a floating-point number. This is often necessary for accurate calculations involving both integers and floats.

Use Purpose
- **Enable Precise Calculations**: Allows integer values to be used in floating-point calculations without truncating results.
- **Avoid Integer Division Truncation**: Converting integers to floats before division prevents loss of decimal places.

Syntax
```
float_var = (float)int_var;
```

Syntax Explanation
- **float_var**: The variable that will store the converted float value.
- **(float)**: Casts the integer to a float type.
- **int_var**: The integer variable to convert.

Simple Code Example
```
int i = 10;
float f = (float)i;   // Converts i to 10.0 in float form
```

Code Example Explanation

- **Converts integer i to float**: Enables f to store 10.0, allowing it to be used in floating-point calculations.

Notes
- Conversion to float does not change the value but changes how it's stored and used in calculations.

Warnings
- Implicitly converting integers to floats in expressions may cause rounding errors in critical calculations.

---

4. Float to Integer Conversion

What is Float to Integer Conversion?
Float-to-integer conversion removes the decimal part of a floating-point number, leaving only the integer portion. This conversion is often used when an integer value is required.

Use Purpose
- **Truncate Decimal Part**: Retains only the integer part of a float.
- **Simplify Calculations**: Converts floating-point results to integers where fractional values are unnecessary.

Syntax

```
int_var = (int)float_var;
```

Syntax Explanation
- **int_var**: The variable that will store the converted integer value.
- **(int)**: Casts the float to an integer type.
- **float_var**: The floating-point variable to convert.

Simple Code Example

```
float f = 2.7;
int i = (int)f;   // Converts f to integer 2
```

Code Example Explanation

- **Truncates f to 2**: The integer i receives only the integer part, discarding the decimal.

Notes
- Truncation removes the fractional part; rounding is not performed.
- Use rounding functions like round() if needed.

Warnings
- Data loss occurs as the fractional component is discarded.

---

5. String to Integer Conversion
What is String to Integer Conversion?
String-to-integer conversion parses a numeric string and returns its integer value. It's commonly used when receiving numeric data as text, like user input or serial data.

Use Purpose
- **Convert Numeric Strings**: Allows numeric strings to be processed as integers in calculations.
- **Parse User Input**: Enables handling of numeric input entered as text.

Syntax
```
int_var = atoi(string_var);
```
Syntax Explanation
- **int_var**: The integer variable to store the converted value.
- **atoi**: Function that converts a string to an integer.
- **string_var**: The string variable containing the numeric value.

Simple Code Example
```
char s[] = "123";
int i = atoi(s);   // Converts string "123" to integer 123
```
Code Example Explanation
- **Converts s to integer**: The string "123" becomes the integer 123, allowing it to be used in calculations.

Notes

- `atoi` returns 0 if the string is non-numeric.
- Use error checking to handle invalid strings.

Warnings

- Converting a non-numeric string results in undefined behavior.

---

6. String to Float Conversion

What is String to Float Conversion?

String-to-float conversion converts a numeric string to a floating-point value. This is useful for processing numeric text that needs to be used in calculations.

Use Purpose

- **Convert Text to Float**: Enables numeric text to be used in floating-point calculations.
- **Handle Sensor Data**: Useful when sensor readings are received as strings.

Syntax

```
float_var = atof(string_var);
```

Syntax Explanation

- **float_var**: The float variable to store the converted value.
- **atof**: Function that converts a string to a float.
- **string_var**: The string containing the numeric value.

Simple Code Example

```
char s[] = "3.14";
float f = atof(s);   // Converts string "3.14" to float 3.14
```

Code Example Explanation

- **Converts s to float**: The string "3.14" becomes the floating-point value 3.14, allowing precise calculations.

Notes

- `atof` does not handle non-numeric strings well; it may return 0.
- Handle errors for non-numeric strings.

Warnings

- Conversion of invalid strings may cause unexpected results.

---

7. Integer to String Conversion

What is Integer to String Conversion?

Integer-to-string conversion allows integer values to be converted into text format. This is often used to display numbers on screens or send numeric data as text.

Use Purpose

- **Display Numbers as Text**: Essential for sending numeric data to displays or serial monitors.
- **Prepare for Text-Based Communication**: Sends integer values as part of string messages.

Syntax

```
sprintf(string_var, "%d", int_var);
```

Syntax Explanation

- **sprintf**: Function to format data into a string.
- **string_var**: The destination string.
- **"%d"**: Format specifier for integers.
- **int_var**: The integer variable to convert.

Simple Code Example

```
int i = 100;
char s[10];
sprintf(s, "%d", i);   // Converts integer 100 to string "100"
```

Code Example Explanation

- **Converts i to string**: Stores "100" in s, making it suitable for display or transmission.

Notes

- The sprintf function is versatile, handling multiple data types.
- Ensure the string buffer is large enough to hold the converted text.

8. Float to String Conversion

What is Float to String Conversion?

Float-to-string conversion transforms a floating-point value into a text format. It's commonly used to display measurements or send data as text.

Use Purpose

- **Display Floating-Point Data**: Useful for showing precise measurements on displays.
- **Prepare Data for Transmission**: Sends floating-point data as part of a string message.

Syntax

```
sprintf(string_var, "%.2f", float_var);
```

Syntax Explanation

- **sprintf**: Function to format data into a string.
- **string_var**: The destination string.
- **"%.2f"**: Format specifier for floats with 2 decimal places.
- **float_var**: The floating-point variable to convert.

Simple Code Example

```
float f = 3.14;
char s[10];
sprintf(s, "%.2f", f);  // Converts float 3.14 to string "3.14"
```

Code Example Explanation

- **Converts f to string**: Stores "3.14" in s, suitable for display or transmission.

Notes

- The %.2f format specifier limits the output to 2 decimal places.
- Adjust decimal places as needed.

Warnings

- Ensure sufficient buffer size to avoid overflow.

Final Project: Sensor Data Conversion and Display

Project Objective

Read a sensor value, convert it to floating-point for calculations, then display it as a string.

Project Circuit (In Table)

Component	Pin Description	Connection Details
STM32 Microcontroller	ADC Channel	Reads sensor voltage
Potentiometer or Sensor	Connected to ADC input	Provides analog data for conversion
LCD or Serial Monitor	Display	Shows converted sensor value

Circuit Analysis

- **ADC Input**: Reads analog voltage from a sensor or potentiometer.
- **Conversion**: Converts ADC reading to float for calculations, then to string for display.

Project Code

```
#include "stm32f4xx_hal.h"
#include <stdio.h>

ADC_HandleTypeDef hadc1;

void ADC_Init(void) {
    __HAL_RCC_ADC1_CLK_ENABLE();
    hadc1.Instance = ADC1;
    hadc1.Init.Resolution = ADC_RESOLUTION_12B;
    HAL_ADC_Init(&hadc1);
}
int main(void) {
    HAL_Init();
    ADC_Init();
    char displayBuffer[20];
```

```
    uint32_t adcValue;
    float voltage;
    while (1) {
        HAL_ADC_Start(&hadc1);
        if (HAL_ADC_PollForConversion(&hadc1, HAL_MAX_DELAY) == HAL_OK)
{
            adcValue = HAL_ADC_GetValue(&hadc1);
            voltage = (float)adcValue * (3.3 / 4095);   // Convert ADC
value to voltage
            sprintf(displayBuffer, "Voltage: %.2f V", voltage);
            // Display `displayBuffer` on LCD or serial monitor
        }
        HAL_Delay(1000);
    }
}
```

Save and Run

1. Save the code as main.c.
2. Compile and upload to the STM32 NUCLEO-F446RE using STM32CubeIDE or Keil.

Check Output

Expected behavior:

- The converted sensor voltage is displayed every second, using both numeric and string conversions.

Summary

This chapter covered various data conversions in C for STM32, including integer-to-float, float-to-integer, and string-to-number conversions. The final project demonstrated how to read sensor data, perform conversions, and display results, highlighting the importance of data conversion in embedded programming.

Control Structures in STM32

Chapter Overview

Control structures are essential components in programming that allow you to control the flow of execution within a program. In embedded systems like the STM32 NUCLEO-F446RE, control structures manage how a program interacts with inputs, processes data, and controls outputs. This chapter covers the fundamental control structures in C, including conditional statements (`if`, `if-else`, `else-if`), loops (`for`, `while`, `do-while`), and `switch` statements.

Chapter Goal

- Understand and apply `if`, `else`, and `else-if` statements for conditional logic.
- Implement `for`, `while`, and `do-while` loops to execute repetitive actions.
- Use `switch` statements to manage multi-option decision-making efficiently.
- Apply control structures in a project to control an LED's state based on button input.

Rules

- **Use `if-else` for Simple Decisions**: Ideal for binary decisions, such as turning an LED on or off based on sensor thresholds.
- **Apply Loops for Repetitive Tasks**: Use `for`, `while`, or `do-while` loops to perform repeated actions, like reading a sensor or generating signals.
- **Implement `switch` for Multi-Option Cases**: A `switch` statement is more efficient than multiple `if` conditions when choosing among several options.
- **Avoid Infinite Loops**: Ensure loops have valid termination conditions to prevent the program from hanging.

- **Optimize Control Structures for Performance**: Efficient control structures help manage processing power and memory, critical in embedded systems.

Syntax Table

Serial No	Topic	Code Snippet	Simple Example
1	If Statement	`if (condition) { statements }`	`if (temp > 25) { LED_ON(); }`
2	If-Else Statement	`if (condition) { statements } else { }`	`if (temp > 25) { LED_ON(); } else { LED_OFF(); }`
3	Else-If Statement	`if (cond1) {} else if (cond2) {}`	`if (temp > 30) {} else if (temp > 20) {}`
4	For Loop	`for (init; cond; update) { statements }`	`for (int i = 0; i < 5; i++) { LED_ON(); }`
5	While Loop	`while (condition) { statements }`	`while (button == 1) { LED_ON(); }`
6	Do-While Loop	`do { statements } while (condition);`	`do { LED_ON(); } while (button == 1);`
7	Switch Statement	`switch (variable) { case value: ... }`	`switch (command) { case 1: LED_ON(); break; }`

Topic Explanations

1. If Statement

What is an If Statement?

An `if` statement is a control structure that executes a block of code only if a specified condition is true. It's essential in embedded systems for making decisions based on sensor readings, button states, or other conditions.

Use Purpose

- **Conditional Execution**: Runs code when a condition is met.
- **Decision-Making**: Allows a program to react dynamically, such as turning on an LED when a temperature exceeds a threshold.

Syntax

```
if (condition) {
    statements;
}
```

Syntax Explanation

- **if**: Keyword that initiates the conditional statement.
- **(condition)**: A logical condition that evaluates to true or false (e.g., `temp > 25`).
- **statements**: Code that executes if the condition is true. Typically enclosed in braces { } for clarity.
- **Condition**: Must be a logical expression resulting in `true` or `false`. Examples include >, <, ==, and logical operators like && (AND) and || (OR).
- **Braces**: Although optional for single statements, using {} improves readability and prevents errors when expanding the code later.

Simple Code Example

```
int temp = 30;
if (temp > 25) {
    LED_ON();  // Turns on the LED if temperature is greater than 25
}
```

Code Example Explanation

- **Evaluates the condition temp > 25**: If temp is greater than 25, LED_ON() is executed to turn on the LED.
- **Skips the code if condition is false**: If temp is not greater than 25, LED_ON() is not executed.

Notes

- Use if statements for single-condition decisions.
- Conditions can be simple or complex and may include multiple logical operators.

Warnings

- Avoid overly complex conditions to keep the code readable and maintainable.

---

2. If-Else Statement

What is an If-Else Statement?

An if-else statement extends the if structure to provide an alternative block of code if the condition is false. This is helpful for binary decisions, such as toggling a device on and off.

Use Purpose

- **Binary Decision-Making**: Executes one block of code if a condition is true and another if it is false.
- **Simple Alternative Actions**: Useful for toggling states based on input conditions.

Syntax

```
if (condition) {
    statements_if_true;
} else {
    statements_if_false;
}
```

Syntax Explanation

- **if**: Initiates the conditional check.
- **else**: Specifies an alternative block of code if the if condition is false.

- **statements_if_true**: Executes if the condition is true.
- **statements_if_false**: Executes if the condition is false.
- **Condition**: Similar to the `if` statement, evaluated to decide which block runs.
- **Else Block**: Runs only if the `if` condition is false. Enclose it in {} to avoid errors when adding more code.

Simple Code Example

```
int temp = 20;
if (temp > 25) {
    LED_ON();   // LED turns on if temp > 25
} else {
    LED_OFF();  // LED turns off if temp <= 25
}
```

Code Example Explanation
- **Turns LED on or off based on temperature**: If `temp` is above 25, the LED turns on; otherwise, it turns off.

Notes
- Use `if-else` for simple binary choices.
- Avoid nesting `if-else` statements excessively to maintain readability.

Warnings
- Keep conditions clear and simple to avoid logical errors.

---

3. Else-If Statement

What is an Else-If Statement?

An `else-if` statement allows checking multiple conditions in sequence. This is useful when there are more than two possible actions to take based on a condition, such as setting different fan speeds based on temperature ranges.

Use Purpose
- **Multi-Condition Decision-Making**: Allows testing multiple conditions in a single structure.

- **Range-Based Actions**: Useful for managing ranges, like adjusting device states based on sensor input.

Syntax

```
if (condition1) {
    statements_if_true1;
} else if (condition2) {
    statements_if_true2;
} else {
    statements_if_all_false;
}
```

Syntax Explanation

- **if**: Checks the first condition.
- **else if**: Additional conditions to check if previous ones are false.
- **else**: Executes if none of the previous conditions are true.
- **statements_if_true1**: Runs if the first condition is true.
- **statements_if_true2**: Runs if the second condition is true.
- **Multiple Conditions**: Allows testing various conditions. The first true condition executes its block, skipping the rest.
- **Final Else**: Optional but useful as a default if no conditions are met.

Simple Code Example

```
int temp = 22;
if (temp > 30) {
    LED_HIGH();
} else if (temp > 20) {
    LED_MEDIUM();
} else {
    LED_LOW();
}
```

Code Example Explanation

- **Adjusts LED brightness based on temperature**: Sets the LED to high, medium, or low brightness based on temperature ranges.

Notes

- Only the first true condition is executed, and the rest are ignored.
- Avoid using too many else if conditions to keep the code efficient.

4. For Loop

What is a For Loop?

A `for` loop repeats a block of code a specific number of times. It's ideal for situations where the number of iterations is known in advance, such as iterating over an array.

Use Purpose

- **Controlled Repetition**: Executes a block of code a fixed number of times.
- **Index-Based Operations**: Useful for looping through arrays or performing repeated actions with a counter.

Syntax

```
for (initialization; condition; update) {
    statements;
}
```

Syntax Explanation

- **for**: The keyword that starts the loop.
- **initialization**: Initializes the loop counter, typically setting it to a starting value.
- **condition**: Checks if the loop should continue running.
- **update**: Modifies the loop counter after each iteration.
- **statements**: Code that executes each time the loop runs.
- **Initialization**: Sets up a loop variable (e.g., `int i = 0`).
- **Condition**: Controls loop termination. If false, the loop exits.
- **Update**: Modifies the loop variable, usually an increment or decrement.

Simple Code Example

```
for (int i = 0; i < 5; i++) {
    LED_TOGGLE();  // Toggles LED five times
}
```

Code Example Explanation

- **Loops five times**: Toggles the LED each time, producing five blinks.

Notes

- Use `for` loops when the iteration count is known.
- `for` loops are useful for repeating actions with a counter.

5. While Loop

What is a While Loop?

A while loop repeats a block of code as long as a specified condition remains true. It's useful for indefinite loops where the number of iterations is not known in advance.

Use Purpose

- **Conditional Repetition**: Continues executing while the condition is true.
- **Real-Time Monitoring**: Suitable for tasks like checking a sensor continuously.

Syntax

```
while (condition) {
    statements;
}
```

Syntax Explanation

- **while**: Starts the loop.
- **condition**: Checks if the loop should continue running. If true, the loop repeats.
- **statements**: Code that executes while the condition is true.
- **Condition**: Evaluated at the beginning of each iteration.
- **Execution**: If true, executes the code block; if false, exits the loop.

Simple Code Example

```
int button = 1;
while (button == 1) {
    LED_ON();   // Keeps LED on while button is pressed
}
```

Code Example Explanation

- **Runs while button == 1**: Turns on the LED as long as the button is pressed.

Notes

- Use while loops for indefinite repetition.
- Ensure there's a way for the condition to become false to prevent infinite loops.

6. Do-While Loop
What is a Do-While Loop?

A do-while loop executes a block of code at least once before checking the condition. It's useful for actions that must run at least once, like prompting for input.

Use Purpose

- **Guaranteed Execution**: Executes code at least once, then repeats based on the condition.
- **Preliminary Action**: Useful for running code that needs at least one execution.

Syntax

```
do {
    statements;
} while (condition);
```

Syntax Explanation

- **do**: Starts the loop, executing the code before checking the condition.
- **statements**: The code that runs each time the loop iterates.
- **while**: Checks the condition after each iteration.
- **Execution**: Runs the statements once before checking the condition.
- **Condition**: If true, the loop repeats; if false, it exits.

Simple Code Example

```
int button;
do {
    button = readButton();
} while (button != 1);
```

Code Example Explanation

- **Reads button at least once**: The loop keeps reading until the button is pressed.

Notes

- The loop always runs at least once, regardless of the initial condition.
- Ideal for menus or input prompts.

7. Switch Statement

What is a Switch Statement?

A `switch` statement evaluates a variable and executes corresponding code based on its value. It's more efficient than multiple `if` statements for choosing among several discrete options.

Use Purpose

- **Multi-Option Decision-Making**: Simplifies handling multiple options.
- **Efficient Selection**: Useful for controlling modes or handling commands.

Syntax

```
switch (variable) {
    case value1:
        statements1;
        break;
    case value2:
        statements2;
        break;
    default:
        statements_default;
}
```

Syntax Explanation

- **switch**: Begins the statement.
- **variable**: The variable to check.
- **case**: Defines a specific value for the variable.
- **statements**: Code that executes if the case matches.
- **break**: Exits the switch to prevent fall-through.
- **default**: Runs if none of the cases match.
- **Cases**: Each case represents a possible value for the variable.
- **Break Statements**: Prevents execution from continuing into the next case.

Simple Code Example

```
int mode = 1;
switch (mode) {
    case 1:
        LED_ON();
        break;
    case 2:
        LED_BLINK();
```

```
        break;
    default:
        LED_OFF();
}
```

Code Example Explanation

- **Controls LED based on mode**: LED either turns on, blinks, or turns off depending on mode's value.

Notes

- `switch` is more efficient than multiple `if-else` statements for multi-option cases.
- `default` is optional but recommended for handling unexpected values.

Warnings

- Forgetting `break` statements can cause unintended fall-through.

Final Project: Button-Controlled LED Pattern

Project Objective

Control an LED based on button input using `if`, `for`, `while`, and `switch` statements.

Project Circuit

Component	Pin Description	Connection Details
STM32 Microcontroller	GPIO Input (Button)	Reads button state
LED	GPIO Output	Controls LED

Project Code

```c
#include "stm32f4xx_hal.h"

#define LED_PIN GPIO_PIN_5

void LED_Init(void) {
    __HAL_RCC_GPIOA_CLK_ENABLE();
    GPIO_InitTypeDef GPIO_InitStruct = {0};
    GPIO_InitStruct.Pin = LED_PIN;
    GPIO_InitStruct.Mode = GPIO_MODE_OUTPUT_PP;
    GPIO_InitStruct.Pull = GPIO_NOPULL;
    GPIO_InitStruct.Speed = GPIO_SPEED_LOW;
    HAL_GPIO_Init(GPIOA, &GPIO_InitStruct);
}

void Button_Init(void) {
    __HAL_RCC_GPIOC_CLK_ENABLE();
    GPIO_InitTypeDef GPIO_InitStruct = {0};
    GPIO_InitStruct.Pin = GPIO_PIN_13;
    GPIO_InitStruct.Mode = GPIO_MODE_INPUT;
    GPIO_InitStruct.Pull = GPIO_PULLUP;
    HAL_GPIO_Init(GPIOC, &GPIO_InitStruct);
}

int main(void) {
    HAL_Init();
    LED_Init();
    Button_Init();

    while (1) {
        int buttonState = HAL_GPIO_ReadPin(GPIOC, GPIO_PIN_13);

        if (buttonState == GPIO_PIN_RESET) {
            for (int i = 0; i < 3; i++) {
                HAL_GPIO_TogglePin(GPIOA, LED_PIN);
                HAL_Delay(500);
            }
        } else {
            HAL_GPIO_WritePin(GPIOA, LED_PIN, GPIO_PIN_RESET);
        }
    }
}
```

Save and Run

1. Save the code as main.c.
2. Compile and upload to the STM32 NUCLEO-F446RE using STM32CubeIDE or Keil.

Check Output

Expected behavior:

- When the button is pressed, the LED blinks three times; otherwise, it remains off.

Arithmetic Operators in STM32

Chapter Overview

Arithmetic operators in C allow for performing mathematical operations, such as addition, subtraction, multiplication, and division. These operations are fundamental in embedded systems, where they are used for tasks like data processing, sensor reading, and control signal generation. This chapter covers the essential arithmetic operators in C, explaining their usage, syntax, and application in STM32 embedded programming.

Chapter Goal

- Understand the main arithmetic operators: addition, subtraction, multiplication, division, and modulus.
- Learn how to apply arithmetic operations to manage and manipulate data.
- Implement arithmetic operators in a practical project that processes sensor input data for display.

Rules

- **Use Appropriate Data Types**: Ensure that the data types used with arithmetic operators support the precision and range required for calculations.
- **Be Cautious with Division and Modulus**: Handle division carefully to avoid division by zero errors. The modulus operator should only be used with integers.
- **Control Overflow in Calculations**: Ensure calculations do not exceed the range of the variable type to avoid unexpected behavior.
- **Optimize for Embedded Systems**: Avoid unnecessary floating-point operations in resource-constrained systems, as they can be more computationally expensive.

- **Use Parentheses for Clarity**: Parentheses improve readability and ensure that complex expressions are evaluated in the correct order.

Syntax Table

Serial No	Topic	Code Snippet	Simple Example
1	Addition Operator (+)	`result = a + b;`	`int sum = 5 + 3;`
2	Subtraction Operator (-)	`result = a - b;`	`int difference = 10 - 4;`
3	Multiplication Operator (*)	`result = a * b;`	`int product = 6 * 7;`
4	Division Operator (/)	`result = a / b;`	`float quotient = 10 / 3.0;`
5	Modulus Operator (%)	`result = a % b;`	`int remainder = 10 % 3;`
6	Increment Operator (++)	`variable++`	`counter++;`
7	Decrement Operator (--)	`variable--`	`counter--;`

Topic Explanations

1. Addition Operator (+)

What is the Addition Operator?

The addition operator (+) sums two operands, returning their total. This operator is commonly used to accumulate values, such as adding measurements from sensors or calculating a total count.

Use Purpose

- **Sum Values**: Combines two values into a single result.
- **Accumulate Data**: Used for totals and accumulated values.

Syntax

```
result = operand1 + operand2;
```

Syntax Explanation

- **result**: The variable that stores the sum.
- **operand1**: The first value to be added.
- **operand2**: The second value to be added.
- **+**: Operator that performs the addition.
- **Operands**: Can be integers, floating-point numbers, or a mix.
- **Result**: Stored in a variable, with its type determining the precision.

Simple Code Example

```
int a = 5;
int b = 3;
int sum = a + b;   // sum is 8
```

Code Example Explanation

- **Adds a and b**: Calculates 5 + 3, storing the result in sum.

Notes

- Addition can overflow if the result exceeds the data type's range.
- Use appropriate data types to handle large sums.

Warnings

- For mixed types (e.g., int and float), the result's type is determined by the larger data type.

2. Subtraction Operator (-)

What is the Subtraction Operator?

The subtraction operator (-) calculates the difference between two operands, returning the result. It's often used in embedded systems to determine the difference between readings or values.

Use Purpose

- **Calculate Differences**: Determines how much one value exceeds another.
- **Control Operations**: Adjust values by a constant or variable amount.

Syntax

```
result = operand1 - operand2;
```

Syntax Explanation

- **result**: The variable that stores the difference.
- **operand1**: The value to be reduced.
- **operand2**: The value to subtract.
- **-**: Operator that performs the subtraction.
- **Operands**: Can be integers, floating-point numbers, or a mix.
- **Result**: Stores the difference based on the operands' types.

Simple Code Example

```
int a = 10;
int b = 4;
int difference = a - b;  // difference is 6
```

Code Example Explanation

- **Subtracts b from a**: Calculates 10 - 4, storing the result in `difference`.

Notes

- Subtraction can result in negative values, which might need specific handling.
- Ensure proper data type to handle the result accurately.

Warnings

- Beware of overflow, especially when subtracting large numbers in unsigned types.

3. Multiplication Operator (*)

What is the Multiplication Operator?

The multiplication operator (*) multiplies two operands, producing their product. It's commonly used to calculate values based on scale factors or to convert units.

Use Purpose

- **Scale Values**: Adjusts a value by a fixed multiplier.
- **Unit Conversion**: Converts values by multiplying by conversion factors.

Syntax

```
result = operand1 * operand2;
```

Syntax Explanation

- **result**: The variable that stores the product.
- **operand1**: The first value to multiply.
- **operand2**: The second value to multiply.
- *****: Operator that performs multiplication.
- **Operands**: Can be integers, floating-point numbers, or a mix.
- **Result**: Depends on operand types and may overflow if operands are too large.

Simple Code Example

```
int a = 6;
int b = 7;
int product = a * b;   // product is 42
```

Code Example Explanation

- **Multiplies a and b**: Calculates 6 * 7, storing the result in `product`.

Notes

- Multiplication results can overflow if they exceed the type's range.
- Floating-point multiplication is slower than integer multiplication.

Warnings

- Large multiplications with integers may require a larger data type to avoid overflow.

4. Division Operator (/)

What is the Division Operator?

The division operator (/) divides one operand by another, returning the quotient. It's commonly used for averaging values, scaling down measurements, or normalizing data.

Use Purpose

- **Calculate Ratios**: Useful for dividing totals into parts.
- **Scale Down Values**: Reduces values by a constant factor.

Syntax

```
result = operand1 / operand2;
```

Syntax Explanation

- **result**: The variable that stores the quotient.
- **operand1**: The dividend or value to divide.
- **operand2**: The divisor or value to divide by.
- **/**: Operator that performs division.
- **Operands**: Can be integers or floats. Integer division discards the remainder.
- **Result**: For integers, the result is truncated; floats provide a decimal result.

Simple Code Example

```
float a = 10.0;
float b = 3.0;
float quotient = a / b;   // quotient is 3.3333
```

Code Example Explanation

- **Divides a by b**: Calculates 10 / 3, resulting in approximately 3.3333.

Notes

- Division by zero causes errors; check the divisor before dividing.
- Integer division discards the remainder, so 10 / 3 would yield 3, not 3.3333.

Warnings

- Avoid division by zero by validating the divisor.

5. Modulus Operator (%)

What is the Modulus Operator?

The modulus operator (%) calculates the remainder when one integer is divided by another. It's used to determine even/odd values or to wrap around counters.

Use Purpose

- **Calculate Remainders**: Determines the leftover part of a division.
- **Control Loop Cycles**: Used for cyclic operations, such as blinking an LED at every other cycle.

Syntax

```
result = operand1 % operand2;
```

Syntax Explanation

- **result**: Stores the remainder.
- **operand1**: The dividend.
- **operand2**: The divisor.
- **%**: Operator that calculates the modulus.
- **Operands**: Must be integers; the result is always an integer.
- **Result**: The remainder after division.

Simple Code Example

```
int a = 10;
int b = 3;
int remainder = a % b;   // remainder is 1
```

Code Example Explanation

- **Calculates remainder of a / b**: 10 % 3 leaves a remainder of 1.

Notes

- Modulus is useful for cyclic operations, like controlling every nth cycle.
- Can only be used with integer types.

Warnings

- Using modulus with zero results in a runtime error.

6. Increment Operator (++)

What is the Increment Operator?

The increment operator (++) increases an integer variable by one. It's commonly used for counters and loops.

Use Purpose

- **Increment Counters**: Adds one to a variable, often in loops.
- **Simplify Code**: Provides a shorthand for `variable = variable + 1`.

Syntax

```
variable++;
```

Syntax Explanation

- **variable**: The variable to increment.
- **++**: Operator that increases the value by 1.
- **Variable**: Must be an integer or similar type.
- **Increment**: Adds 1 to the variable's current value.

Simple Code Example

```
int counter = 0;
counter++;  // counter is now 1
```

Code Example Explanation

- **Increases counter by 1**: Each `counter++` adds 1 to `counter`.

Notes

- `++variable` increments before returning the value, while `variable++` increments after.
- Commonly used in loops, such as `for` loops.

Warnings

- Using increment on non-integer types may lead to unexpected behavior.

7. Decrement Operator (--)

What is the Decrement Operator?

The decrement operator (--) decreases an integer variable by one. It's used to reduce counters or for reverse iteration in loops.

Use Purpose

- **Decrement Counters**: Subtracts one from a variable.
- **Simplify Code**: Provides a shorthand for `variable = variable - 1`.

Syntax

```
variable--;
```

Syntax Explanation

- **variable**: The variable to decrement.
- **--**: Operator that decreases the value by 1.
- **Variable**: Must be an integer or similar type.
- **Decrement**: Subtracts 1 from the current value.

Simple Code Example

```
int counter = 5;
counter--;   // counter is now 4
```

Code Example Explanation

- **Decreases counter by 1**: Each `counter--` subtracts 1 from `counter`.

Notes

- `--variable` decrements before returning, while `variable--` decrements after.
- Common in reverse loops or countdowns.

Warnings

- Using decrement on unsigned variables can cause underflow.

Final Project: Sensor Data Processing with Arithmetic Operators

Project Objective

Use arithmetic operators to read sensor data, scale it to voltage, and display the result.

Project Circuit

Component	Pin Description	Connection Details
STM32 Microcontroller	ADC Channel	Reads sensor data as an analog voltage
Potentiometer or Sensor	Connected to ADC input	Provides input data for processing
LCD or Serial Monitor	Display	Shows the processed sensor value

Project Code

```
#include "stm32f4xx_hal.h"
#include <stdio.h>

ADC_HandleTypeDef hadc1;

void ADC_Init(void) {
    __HAL_RCC_ADC1_CLK_ENABLE();
    hadc1.Instance = ADC1;
    hadc1.Init.Resolution = ADC_RESOLUTION_12B;
    HAL_ADC_Init(&hadc1);
}

int main(void) {
    HAL_Init();
    ADC_Init();

    uint32_t adcValue;
    float voltage;
    char displayBuffer[20];

    while (1) {
        HAL_ADC_Start(&hadc1);
        if (HAL_ADC_PollForConversion(&hadc1, HAL_MAX_DELAY) == HAL_OK)
{
            adcValue = HAL_ADC_GetValue(&hadc1);
```

```
            voltage = (adcValue * 3.3) / 4095;  // Scale ADC value to
voltage
            sprintf(displayBuffer, "Voltage: %.2f V", voltage);
            // Display `displayBuffer` on LCD or serial monitor
        }
        HAL_Delay(1000);
    }
}
```

Save and Run

1. Save the code as `main.c`.
2. Compile and upload to the STM32 NUCLEO-F446RE using STM32CubeIDE or Keil.

Check Output

Expected behavior:

- The scaled sensor voltage is displayed every second, demonstrating the use of arithmetic operators for data processing.

Summary

This chapter covered the primary arithmetic operators in C for STM32 programming, including addition, subtraction, multiplication, division, and modulus. The final project demonstrated how to process sensor data using arithmetic operators, providing practical insights into their application in embedded systems.

Comparison Operators in STM32

Chapter Overview

Comparison operators are fundamental in programming, allowing the program to evaluate relationships between values, such as equality, greater than, or less than. In embedded systems, comparison operators play a key role in conditional statements and decision-making, enabling responses to sensor inputs, user commands, or system states. This chapter covers the main comparison operators in C, their usage, syntax, and practical applications in STM32 embedded programming.

Chapter Goal

- Understand and use comparison operators: equal to, not equal to, greater than, less than, greater than or equal to, and less than or equal to.
- Learn how to implement comparison operations within conditional structures.
- Apply comparison operators in a practical project for controlling an LED based on sensor data.

Rules

- **Use Comparison Operators in Conditions**: Comparison operators are typically used in if, while, or for conditions to evaluate relationships between values.
- **Be Mindful of Data Types**: Ensure the variables being compared are of compatible types to avoid unexpected behavior.
- **Understand Operator Precedence**: Comparison operators have lower precedence than arithmetic operators, so use parentheses to clarify complex conditions.
- **Avoid Unintended Assignments in Conditions**: Use == for comparison, not =, which is an assignment operator.

- **Check for Boundary Conditions**: For ranges, use >= and <= to include boundary values as needed.

Syntax Table

Serial No	Operator	Code Snippet	Simple Example
1	Equal To (==)	`if (a == b) { statements; }`	`if (temp == 25) { LED_ON(); }`
2	Not Equal To (!=)	`if (a != b) { statements; }`	`if (temp != 25) { LED_OFF(); }`
3	Greater Than (>)	`if (a > b) { statements; }`	`if (temp > 25) { FAN_ON(); }`
4	Less Than (<)	`if (a < b) { statements; }`	`if (temp < 15) { HEATER_ON(); }`
5	Greater Than or Equal (>=)	`if (a >= b) { statements; }`	`if (temp >= 20) { LED_ON(); }`
6	Less Than or Equal (<=)	`if (a <= b) { statements; }`	`if (temp <= 10) { LED_OFF(); }`

Topic Explanations

1. Equal To (==)

What is the Equal To Operator?

The == operator checks if two values are equal, returning true if they are the same. In embedded systems, this is often used to check sensor values or to see if a condition has been met.

Use Purpose

- **Check for Equality**: Used to confirm if two values are the same.
- **Condition Testing**: Commonly used in `if` statements to trigger actions when values match.

Syntax

```
if (operand1 == operand2) {
    statements;
}
```

Syntax Explanation

- **operand1**: The first value or variable being compared.
- **==**: The equality operator, which checks if `operand1` and `operand2` are equal.
- **operand2**: The second value or variable for comparison.
- **Operands**: Can be integers, floating-point numbers, or characters.
- **Condition**: Evaluates to true if the two operands are equal, executing the code inside { }.

Simple Code Example

```
int temp = 25;
if (temp == 25) {
    LED_ON();  // Turns on LED if temp is equal to 25
}
```

Code Example Explanation

- **Compares `temp` to 25**: If `temp` is 25, the LED is turned on.

Notes

- Always use == for comparison, not =, which assigns values.
- Comparison can be used with different types, but ensure compatibility.

Warnings

- Accidental use of = in place of == can lead to logical errors.

---

2. Not Equal To (!=)

What is the Not Equal To Operator?

The ! = operator checks if two values are different, returning true if they are not equal. This is often used in embedded systems to perform actions when a specific condition is not met.

Use Purpose

- **Check for Inequality**: Confirms that two values are not the same.
- **Inverse Conditions**: Useful when you want to ensure a variable is not equal to a certain value.

Syntax

```
if (operand1 != operand2) {
    statements;
}
```

Syntax Explanation

- **operand1**: The first value or variable in the comparison.
- **!=**: The inequality operator, which checks if operand1 is not equal to operand2.
- **operand2**: The second value or variable for comparison.
- **Operands**: Can be of various types (integers, floats, chars).
- **Condition**: True if operand1 and operand2 are different, running the code in { }.

Simple Code Example

```
int temp = 20;
if (temp != 25) {
    LED_OFF();   // Turns off LED if temp is not 25
}
```

Code Example Explanation

- **Checks if temp is not 25**: If temp is any value other than 25, the LED turns off.

Notes

- Useful for triggering code only when two values are not equal.
- Check for type compatibility to avoid unexpected results.

Warnings

- Using ! = with floating-point numbers can be inaccurate due to precision issues.

3. Greater Than (>)

What is the Greater Than Operator?

The > operator checks if one value is greater than another. It's commonly used in embedded systems to take action when a sensor reading exceeds a threshold.

Use Purpose

- **Threshold Checking**: Triggers actions when a value exceeds a predefined limit.
- **Comparison in Loops**: Often used in loops for counting or monitoring variables.

Syntax

```
if (operand1 > operand2) {
    statements;
}
```

Syntax Explanation

- **operand1**: The value to check if it is greater than operand2.
- **>**: The greater than operator, which evaluates if operand1 is larger than operand2.
- **operand2**: The value being compared.
- **Operands**: Must be compatible types.
- **Condition**: Executes the block if operand1 is indeed greater than operand2.

Simple Code Example

```
int temp = 30;
if (temp > 25) {
    FAN_ON();   // Turns on the fan if temp exceeds 25
}
```

Code Example Explanation

- **Checks if temp is greater than 25**: If true, the fan turns on.

Notes

- Use > to test if a value has crossed a threshold.
- Integer comparisons are faster than floating-point comparisons in embedded systems.

Warnings

- Ensure operand types match to avoid implicit conversions and errors.

4. Less Than (<)

What is the Less Than Operator?

The < operator checks if one value is less than another. It is useful in embedded systems for checking if a reading falls below a safe level or threshold.

Use Purpose

- **Lower Bound Checking**: Triggers actions when a value is below a specified limit.
- **Range Checks**: Used in conjunction with > to test if values fall within a specific range.

Syntax

```
if (operand1 < operand2) {
    statements;
}
```

Syntax Explanation

- **operand1**: The value to check if it is less than operand2.
- **<**: The less than operator, which evaluates if operand1 is smaller than operand2.
- **operand2**: The value to compare.
- **Operands**: Should be of compatible types to prevent unexpected results.
- **Condition**: True if operand1 is less than operand2, executing the code in { }.

Simple Code Example

```
int temp = 10;
if (temp < 15) {
    HEATER_ON();   // Turns on heater if temp is below 15
}
```

Code Example Explanation

- **Checks if temp is less than 15**: If true, the heater turns on.

Notes

- Useful for lower threshold checks, like minimum safe values.
- Often used in range checks along with the > operator.

5. Greater Than or Equal To (>=)

What is the Greater Than or Equal To Operator?

The >= operator checks if one value is greater than or equal to another, ensuring that the value meets or exceeds a specified level.

Use Purpose

- **Inclusive Upper Bound**: Checks if a value is above or exactly at a threshold.
- **Range Validation**: Ensures a variable meets a minimum requirement.

Syntax

```
if (operand1 >= operand2) {
    statements;
}
```

Syntax Explanation

- **operand1**: The first value to compare.
- **>=**: The greater than or equal operator, which checks if operand1 is greater than or equal to operand2.
- **operand2**: The second value to compare.
- **Operands**: Compatible data types are required.
- **Condition**: Executes code if operand1 is at least as large as operand2.

Simple Code Example

```
int temp = 20;
if (temp >= 20) {
    LED_ON();  // Turns on LED if temp is 20 or more
}
```

Code Example Explanation

- **Checks if temp is at least 20**: If true, the LED turns on.

Notes

- Use >= for inclusive checks where the boundary value is part of the range.
- Be mindful of the range and type compatibility for accurate results.

Warnings

- Misusing signed and unsigned types together can lead to unexpected results.

6. Less Than or Equal To (<=)

What is the Less Than or Equal To Operator?

The <= operator checks if one value is less than or equal to another, ensuring the value does not exceed a specific upper limit.

Use Purpose

- **Inclusive Lower Bound**: Verifies that a value is within or below a maximum.
- **Range Enforcement**: Used in range validations to confirm a variable remains within bounds.

Syntax

```
if (operand1 <= operand2) {
    statements;
}
```

Syntax Explanation

- **operand1**: The first value to compare.
- **<=**: The less than or equal operator, which checks if operand1 is less than or equal to operand2.
- **operand2**: The second value to compare.
- **Operands**: Should be compatible to avoid implicit type conversions.
- **Condition**: Executes if operand1 does not exceed operand2.

Simple Code Example

```
int temp = 10;
if (temp <= 10) {
    LED_OFF();   // Turns off LED if temp is 10 or less
}
```

Code Example Explanation

- **Checks if temp is 10 or lower**: If true, the LED turns off.

Notes

- Use <= for boundary-inclusive checks, such as ensuring values remain within limits.
- Typically used to confirm values are within an upper constraint.

Warnings

- Comparing signed and unsigned variables can produce unexpected results.

Final Project: LED Control Based on Temperature Range

Project Objective

Control an LED based on temperature readings from a sensor, using comparison operators to turn the LED on, blink, or off within specific temperature ranges.

Project Circuit

Component	Pin Description	Connection Details
STM32 Microcontroller	ADC Channel	Reads temperature sensor data
Temperature Sensor	Connected to ADC input	Provides temperature reading
LED	GPIO Output	Indicates temperature state

Project Code

```
#include "stm32f4xx_hal.h"

ADC_HandleTypeDef hadc1;

void ADC_Init(void) {
    __HAL_RCC_ADC1_CLK_ENABLE();
    hadc1.Instance = ADC1;
    hadc1.Init.Resolution = ADC_RESOLUTION_12B;
    HAL_ADC_Init(&hadc1);
}

void LED_Control(int temp) {
    if (temp >= 30) {
        LED_HIGH();     // LED at high brightness if temp >= 30
    } else if (temp >= 20) {
        LED_MEDIUM();   // LED at medium brightness if temp is 20-29
    } else {
        LED_LOW();      // LED at low brightness if temp < 20
    }
}

int main(void) {
    HAL_Init();
```

```
ADC_Init();

uint32_t adcValue;
int temp;

while (1) {
    HAL_ADC_Start(&hadc1);
    if (HAL_ADC_PollForConversion(&hadc1, HAL_MAX_DELAY) == HAL_OK)
{

        adcValue = HAL_ADC_GetValue(&hadc1);
        temp = (adcValue * 100) / 4095;  // Convert ADC value to
temperature estimate
        LED_Control(temp);
    }
    HAL_Delay(1000);
}
}
```

Save and Run

1. Save the code as main.c.
2. Compile and upload to the STM32 NUCLEO-F446RE using STM32CubeIDE or Keil.

Check Output

Expected behavior:

- LED brightness changes based on the temperature, using different comparison operators to control the output.

Summary

This chapter covered the essential comparison operators in C programming for STM32, including equal to, not equal to, greater than, less than, greater than or equal, and less than or equal. The final project demonstrated how to use these operators in a practical application, showing how they control system behavior based on sensor data.

Boolean Operators in STM32

Chapter Overview

Boolean operators allow logical operations to be performed on expressions, enabling complex decision-making within a program. In embedded systems, Boolean operators are crucial for evaluating multiple conditions simultaneously, such as checking multiple sensor thresholds or handling input from various buttons. This chapter covers the primary Boolean operators (AND, OR, and NOT), their syntax, and their practical use in STM32 embedded programming.

Chapter Goal

- Understand and use the main Boolean operators: AND (&&), OR (||), and NOT (!).
- Learn how to combine Boolean operators to create complex logical expressions.
- Implement Boolean logic in a practical project to control an LED based on multiple sensor conditions.

Rules

- **Use AND to Check Multiple Conditions**: Use the && operator to ensure that all conditions are true.
- **Use OR for Alternative Conditions**: Use the || operator to allow actions if any of the conditions are true.
- **Apply NOT to Invert Conditions**: Use the ! operator to reverse the logical state of a condition.
- **Control Operator Precedence with Parentheses**: Use parentheses to clarify and control the order of evaluation in complex expressions.
- **Avoid Complex Expressions in Conditions**: Keep expressions simple to maintain readability and prevent errors.

Syntax Table

Serial No	Operator	Code Snippet	Simple Example
1	AND (&&)	`if (cond1 && cond2) { statements; }`	`if (temp > 25 && humidity < 50) { LED_ON(); }`
3	NOT (!)	`if (!condition) { statements; }`	`if (!doorClosed) { LED_BLINK(); }`

Topic Explanations

1. AND Operator (&&)

What is the AND Operator?

The && (AND) operator is a Boolean operator that evaluates to true only if both conditions are true. In embedded systems, && is useful for ensuring that multiple criteria are met before executing a specific action, such as turning on a fan only when both temperature and humidity exceed certain thresholds.

Use Purpose

- **Check Multiple Conditions**: Ensures that all specified conditions are true.
- **Control System Responses**: Used for actions that require multiple parameters, like checking sensor values.

Syntax

```
if (condition1 && condition2) {
    statements;
}
```

Syntax Explanation

- **condition1**: The first logical expression to evaluate.
- **&&**: The AND operator, which requires both condition1 and condition2 to be true.

- **condition2**: The second logical expression to evaluate.
- **Operands**: Can be variables, expressions, or function calls that return a boolean result.
- **Result**: The statement block executes only if both conditions are true.

Simple Code Example

```
int temp = 30;
int humidity = 40;
if (temp > 25 && humidity < 50) {
    LED_ON();   // Turns on LED if temp > 25 and humidity < 50
}
```

Code Example Explanation

- **Checks if both temp is greater than 25 and humidity is less than 50**: Only if both conditions are true does the LED turn on.

Notes

- Use && to combine conditions that must all be true for the action to execute.
- Combine multiple && operators to check more than two conditions.

Warnings

- Avoid overly complex expressions to maintain readability.
- Ensure all conditions are valid and won't cause side effects.

---

2. OR Operator (||)

What is the OR Operator?

The || (OR) operator is a Boolean operator that evaluates to true if at least one of the specified conditions is true. In embedded systems, the OR operator is used to trigger actions when any one of multiple conditions is met, such as activating an alarm if either temperature or pressure exceeds a safe threshold.

Use Purpose

- **Alternative Condition Checking**: Allows actions if one or more conditions are met.
- **Set Multiple Triggers**: Useful for monitoring various inputs or sensors.

Syntax

```
if (condition1 || condition2) {
    statements;
}
```

Syntax Explanation

- **condition1**: The first condition to evaluate.
- **||**: The OR operator, which returns true if either `condition1` or `condition2` is true.
- **condition2**: The second condition to evaluate.
- **Operands**: Typically variables, expressions, or functions returning boolean results.
- **Result**: The statement block executes if at least one of the conditions is true.

Simple Code Example

```
int button1 = 1;
int button2 = 0;
if (button1 == 1 || button2 == 1) {
    LED_TOGGLE();  // Toggles LED if either button1 or button2 is pressed
}
```

Code Example Explanation

- **Checks if either button1 or button2 is pressed**: The LED toggles if any of the buttons are pressed.

Notes

- Use || for conditions where any one of several triggers will execute the action.
- Combine multiple || operators to check more than two conditions.

Warnings

- Be cautious with || in complex expressions, as it can lead to unintended results.
- Ensure conditions are simple for readability and maintainability.

3. NOT Operator (!)

What is the NOT Operator?

The ! (NOT) operator reverses the truth value of a condition. If the condition is true, ! makes it false, and if it is false, ! makes it true. In embedded systems, ! is used to check if a condition is not met, such as verifying that a switch is not pressed before turning on an LED.

Use Purpose

- **Invert Condition**: Used when the action should occur only if the condition is false.
- **Check Negative Conditions**: Useful for checking if a state is inactive or a condition is unmet.

Syntax

```
if (!condition) {
    statements;
}
```

Syntax Explanation

- **!**: The NOT operator, which inverts the result of the condition.
- **condition**: The condition to be inverted.
- **Operand**: A boolean condition or variable.
- **Result**: The statement block executes only if the condition is false.

Simple Code Example

```
int doorClosed = 0;
if (!doorClosed) {
    LED_BLINK();   // Blinks LED if door is not closed
}
```

Code Example Explanation

- **Checks if doorClosed is false (0)**: If doorClosed is false, the LED blinks.

Notes

- Use ! to simplify code where actions are required if a condition is not true.
- Ideal for checking flags or status indicators.

Final Project: LED Control Based on Multiple Sensor Conditions

Project Objective

Control an LED based on readings from multiple sensors, using Boolean operators to manage complex conditions.

Project Circuit

Component	Pin Description	Connection Details
STM32 Microcontroller	GPIO Input (Sensors)	Reads input from temperature and humidity sensors
LED	GPIO Output	Indicates conditions met

Project Code

```
#include "stm32f4xx_hal.h"

ADC_HandleTypeDef hadc1;

void ADC_Init(void) {
    __HAL_RCC_ADC1_CLK_ENABLE();
    hadc1.Instance = ADC1;
    hadc1.Init.Resolution = ADC_RESOLUTION_12B;
    HAL_ADC_Init(&hadc1);
}

void LED_Control(int temp, int humidity) {
    if (temp > 25 && humidity < 50) {
        LED_ON();        // Turns on LED if temp > 25 and humidity < 50
    } else if (temp > 30 || humidity > 60) {
        LED_BLINK();     // Blinks LED if temp > 30 or humidity > 60
    } else if (!temp) {
        LED_OFF();       // Turns off LED if temp is zero (an error
condition)
    }
}

int main(void) {
    HAL_Init();
    ADC_Init();

    uint32_t tempValue, humidityValue;
    int temp, humidity;
```

```
    while (1) {
        HAL_ADC_Start(&hadc1);
        if (HAL_ADC_PollForConversion(&hadc1, HAL_MAX_DELAY) == HAL_OK)
{
            tempValue = HAL_ADC_GetValue(&hadc1);
            temp = (tempValue * 100) / 4095;  // Convert ADC value to
temperature

            // Assuming a second ADC channel or conversion for humidity
            humidityValue = HAL_ADC_GetValue(&hadc1);
            humidity = (humidityValue * 100) / 4095;  // Convert ADC to
humidity

            LED_Control(temp, humidity);
        }
        HAL_Delay(1000);
    }
}
```

Save and Run

1. Save the code as `main.c`.
2. Compile and upload to the STM32 NUCLEO-F446RE using STM32CubeIDE or Keil.

Check Output

Expected behavior:

- The LED turns on, blinks, or turns off based on various sensor conditions, demonstrating the use of Boolean operators to control complex logic.

Summary

This chapter covered the essential Boolean operators in C programming for STM32, including AND (&&), OR (||), and NOT (!). These operators enable complex condition checking and decision-making in embedded applications. The final project demonstrated the use of Boolean logic for controlling an LED based on multiple sensor readings, highlighting how Boolean operators enable flexible, multi-condition responses in embedded systems.

Compound Operators in STM32

Chapter Overview

Compound operators combine arithmetic and assignment operations, allowing efficient manipulation of variables in a single step. These operators help simplify code, reduce redundancy, and improve readability in embedded systems, where concise and clear code is critical. This chapter covers the essential compound operators in C, explains their syntax, and demonstrates their application in STM32 programming.

Chapter Goal

- Understand and use the main compound operators: addition assignment (+=), subtraction assignment (-=), multiplication assignment (*=), division assignment (/=), and modulus assignment (%=).
- Learn how compound operators can simplify code by reducing repetitive expressions.
- Apply compound operators in a practical project to manage sensor data processing and LED control.

Rules

- **Use Compound Operators for Efficiency**: Simplify expressions by combining operations and assignments.
- **Understand Data Type Limitations**: Ensure variables used with compound operators can handle the result to avoid overflow or underflow.
- **Control Calculation Order with Parentheses**: Compound operators follow standard arithmetic rules but may benefit from parentheses for clarity.
- **Be Cautious with Division and Modulus**: Handle division and modulus carefully to avoid division by zero errors.

Syntax Table

Serial No	Operator	Code Snippet	Simple Example
1	Addition Assignment (+=)	`variable += value;`	`counter += 5; //` Adds 5 to counter
2	Subtraction Assignment (-=)	`variable -= value;`	`timer -= 2; //` Subtracts 2 from timer
3	Multiplication Assignment (*=)	`variable *= value;`	`area *= 3; //` Multiplies area by 3
4	Division Assignment (/=)	`variable /= value;`	`average /= count; //` Divides average by count
5	Modulus Assignment (%=)	`variable %= value;`	`counter %= 4; //` Sets counter to remainder of counter/4

Topic Explanations

1. Addition Assignment (+=)

What is the Addition Assignment Operator?

The addition assignment operator (+=) adds a specified value to a variable and assigns the result to that variable. This is commonly used in embedded systems to increment counters, accumulate sensor readings, or manage time intervals.

Use Purpose

- **Efficient Accumulation**: Adds a value to a variable without needing an extra line.
- **Simplifies Incrementing**: Reduces repetitive expressions in counter-based operations.

Syntax

```
variable += value;
```

Syntax Explanation

- **variable**: The variable that stores the result.
- **+=**: The addition assignment operator, which adds `value` to `variable`.
- **value**: The amount to add to `variable`.
- **Operands**: `variable` is updated by adding `value` to its current value.
- **Result**: Stored in `variable` after addition.

Simple Code Example

```
int counter = 10;
counter += 5;   // counter is now 15
```

Code Example Explanation

- **Adds 5 to counter**: The new value of `counter` is 15, replacing the original value.

Notes

- += is useful for accumulating totals in loops or repetitive calculations.
- Often used in place of `variable = variable + value`.

Warnings

- Ensure `value` doesn't cause overflow or underflow in `variable`.

2. Subtraction Assignment (-=)

What is the Subtraction Assignment Operator?

The subtraction assignment operator (-=) subtracts a specified value from a variable and assigns the result to that variable. This operator is used for countdowns, timers, and decrementing values in embedded systems.

Use Purpose

- **Efficient Decrementing**: Subtracts a value from a variable in a single step.
- **Simplifies Code**: Reduces redundancy in decrementing expressions.

Syntax

```
variable -= value;
```

Syntax Explanation

- **variable**: The variable that stores the result.
- **-=**: The subtraction assignment operator, which subtracts value from variable.
- **value**: The amount to subtract from variable.
- **Operands**: variable is reduced by value.
- **Result**: Stored in variable after subtraction.

Simple Code Example

```
int timer = 20;
timer -= 3;  // timer is now 17
```

Code Example Explanation

- **Subtracts 3 from timer**: The new value of timer is 17, replacing the original value.

Notes

- -= is commonly used in countdowns and timing loops.
- Useful for decreasing values in a concise manner.

Warnings

- Ensure value does not reduce variable below an acceptable threshold.

3. Multiplication Assignment (*=)

What is the Multiplication Assignment Operator?

The multiplication assignment operator (*=) multiplies a variable by a specified value and assigns the result to that variable. This is useful in scaling values, such as converting units or adjusting sensor data.

Use Purpose

- **Efficient Scaling**: Scales a variable by a multiplier without needing extra code.
- **Simplifies Multiplication**: Useful for adjusting values or performing unit conversions.

Syntax

```
variable *= value;
```

Syntax Explanation

- **variable**: The variable to store the result.
- ***=**: The multiplication assignment operator, which multiplies variable by value.
- **value**: The multiplier.
- **Operands**: variable is multiplied by value.
- **Result**: Stored in variable after multiplication.

Simple Code Example

```
int area = 5;
area *= 4;   // area is now 20
```

Code Example Explanation

- **Multiplies area by 4**: The new value of area is 20.

Notes

- Useful for scaling data, such as sensor conversions or adjusting calculations.
- Often replaces variable = variable * value.

Warnings

- Be cautious of overflow when multiplying large numbers.

4. Division Assignment (/=)

What is the Division Assignment Operator?

The division assignment operator (/=) divides a variable by a specified value and assigns the result to that variable. It is commonly used to average values or reduce values by a factor.

Use Purpose

- **Efficient Reduction**: Reduces a variable by a divisor in a single step.
- **Simplifies Averaging**: Commonly used for calculating averages or scaling down values.

Syntax

```
variable /= value;
```

Syntax Explanation

- **variable**: The variable to store the result.
- **/=**: The division assignment operator, which divides variable by value.
- **value**: The divisor.
- **Operands**: variable is divided by value.
- **Result**: Stored in variable after division.

Simple Code Example

```
int total = 50;
total /= 5;  // total is now 10
```

Code Example Explanation

- **Divides total by 5**: The new value of total is 10.

Notes

- total /= count; is often used to compute averages by dividing the total by a count.
- Replaces variable = variable / value.

Warnings

- Avoid division by zero by checking the divisor.

5. Modulus Assignment (%=)

What is the Modulus Assignment Operator?

The modulus assignment operator (%=) calculates the remainder of a variable divided by a specified value and assigns the result to that variable. It's commonly used for cyclic counters or implementing periodic actions.

Use Purpose

- **Calculate Remainders**: Reduces a variable to a remainder in a single step.
- **Simplify Cyclic Operations**: Useful for creating loops that reset periodically.

Syntax

```
variable %= value;
```

Syntax Explanation

- **variable**: The variable to store the remainder.
- **%=**: The modulus assignment operator, which calculates `variable % value`.
- **value**: The divisor.
- **Operands**: Must be integers for modulus to be meaningful.
- **Result**: `variable` stores the remainder after division by `value`.

Simple Code Example

```
int counter = 10;
counter %= 3;  // counter is now 1
```

Code Example Explanation

- **Calculates remainder of `counter / 3`**: The new value of `counter` is 1, as 10 divided by 3 leaves a remainder of 1.

Notes

- `counter %= max;` can implement cyclic counters that reset when they reach a maximum.
- Ideal for managing periodic tasks in loops.

Warnings

- Using modulus with zero will result in a runtime error.

Final Project: Sensor Data Processing with Compound Operators

Project Objective

Process real-time sensor data using compound operators to update values, calculate averages, and control an LED based on thresholds.

Project Circuit

Component	Pin Description	Connection Details
STM32 Microcontroller	ADC Channel	Reads data from temperature sensor
Temperature Sensor	Connected to ADC input	Provides temperature data
LED	GPIO Output	Indicates if temperature exceeds threshold

Project Code

```
#include "stm32f4xx_hal.h"
ADC_HandleTypeDef hadc1;
void ADC_Init(void) {
    __HAL_RCC_ADC1_CLK_ENABLE();
    hadc1.Instance = ADC1;
    hadc1.Init.Resolution = ADC_RESOLUTION_12B;
    HAL_ADC_Init(&hadc1);
}
void LED_Control(int temp) {
    if (temp >= 30) {
        LED_ON();
    } else {
        LED_OFF();
    }
}
int main(void) {
    HAL_Init();
    ADC_Init();
    uint32_t adcValue;
    int temp;
    int totalTemp = 0;
```

```
    int sampleCount = 0;

    while (1) {
        HAL_ADC_Start(&hadc1);
        if (HAL_ADC_PollForConversion(&hadc1, HAL_MAX_DELAY) == HAL_OK)
{
            adcValue = HAL_ADC_GetValue(&hadc1);
            temp = (adcValue * 100) / 4095;  // Convert ADC to
temperature

            // Update totalTemp and sampleCount using compound
operators
            totalTemp += temp;
            sampleCount += 1;

            if (sampleCount == 10) {  // Every 10 samples, calculate
the average
                int averageTemp = totalTemp / sampleCount;
                LED_Control(averageTemp);  // Control LED based on
average temperature

                // Reset totalTemp and sampleCount
                totalTemp = 0;
                sampleCount = 0;
            }
        }
        HAL_Delay(1000);
    }
}
```

Save and Run

1. Save the code as `main.c`.
2. Compile and upload to the STM32 NUCLEO-F446RE using STM32CubeIDE or Keil.

Check Output

- The LED is controlled based on the average temperature calculated every 10 samples, using compound operators to manage data accumulation and reset.

Summary

This chapter covered essential compound operators in C for STM32 programming, including addition assignment, subtraction assignment, multiplication assignment, division assignment, and modulus assignment. Compound operators help simplify calculations and improve code readability in embedded systems. The final project demonstrated how to use compound operators to manage sensor data processing and control an LED based on temperature thresholds.

Bitwise Operators in STM32

Chapter Overview

Bitwise operators allow manipulation of individual bits within a variable, which is particularly useful in embedded systems where efficient data processing is essential. Bitwise operations are commonly used to control hardware, manage flags, and perform low-level data manipulation. This chapter covers the essential bitwise operators in C, explaining their usage, syntax, and practical application in STM32 programming.

Chapter Goal

- Understand and use the main bitwise operators: AND (&), OR (|), XOR (^), NOT (~), left shift (<<), and right shift (>>).
- Learn how to manipulate individual bits for tasks like setting, clearing, toggling, and checking specific bits.
- Apply bitwise operations in a practical project to control an LED matrix based on specific bit patterns.

Rules

- **Use Bitwise AND to Mask Bits**: Apply the & operator to clear or isolate specific bits.
- **Apply Bitwise OR to Set Bits**: Use | to turn on specific bits without affecting others.
- **Use XOR to Toggle Bits**: Apply ^ to flip bits from 0 to 1 or from 1 to 0.
- **Use Shifts for Efficient Multiplication and Division**: Left shift (<<) to multiply by powers of 2, right shift (>>) to divide.
- **Control Operator Precedence with Parentheses**: Use parentheses in complex expressions to ensure correct order of operations.

Syntax Table

Serial No	Operator	Code Snippet	Simple Example
1	AND (&)	`result = a & b;`	`mask = value & 0x0F;`
3	XOR (^)	`result = a ^ b;`	`toggle = state ^ 0x01;`
4	NOT (~)	`result = ~a;`	`inverted = ~value;`
5	Left Shift (<<)	`result = a << n;`	`shifted = value << 2;`
6	Right Shift (>>)	`result = a >> n;`	`shifted = value >> 3;`

Topic Explanations

1. Bitwise AND (&)

What is the Bitwise AND Operator?

The bitwise AND operator (&) performs a binary AND operation between corresponding bits of two operands. It's commonly used to mask bits, clearing unwanted bits while keeping specific bits intact.

Use Purpose

- **Masking**: Clears bits selectively to isolate specific parts of a value.
- **Bit Checking**: Checks if specific bits are set by masking all other bits.

Syntax

```
result = operand1 & operand2;
```

Syntax Explanation

- **result**: Stores the outcome of the bitwise AND operation.
- **operand1**: The first value.
- **&**: The AND operator, which sets each bit in `result` to 1 if both corresponding bits in `operand1` and `operand2` are 1.
- **operand2**: The second value.
- **Operands**: Often used with hexadecimal masks to isolate specific bits.
- **Result**: Each bit in `result` is 1 only if the corresponding bits in both operands are 1.

Simple Code Example

```
int value = 0b10101101;
int mask = 0b00001111;
int result = value & mask;   // result is 0b00001101
```

Code Example Explanation

- **Applies mask to value**: Only the last four bits are retained; the rest are cleared.

Notes

- & is commonly used to clear bits by applying a mask.
- Often used to check the status of specific bits.

Warnings

- Be cautious with mask values to avoid clearing unintended bits.

---

2. Bitwise OR (|)

What is the Bitwise OR Operator?

The bitwise OR operator (|) performs a binary OR operation between corresponding bits of two operands. It's used to set specific bits without affecting other bits in a variable.

Use Purpose

- **Setting Bits**: Turns on specific bits while leaving others unchanged.
- **Combining Flags**: Used to combine multiple binary flags.

Syntax

```
result = operand1 | operand2;
```

Syntax Explanation

- **result**: Stores the outcome of the bitwise OR operation.
- **operand1**: The first value.
- **|**: The OR operator, which sets each bit in result to 1 if either corresponding bit in operand1 or operand2 is 1.
- **operand2**: The second value.
- **Operands**: Can be variables, literals, or masks.
- **Result**: Each bit in result is 1 if either bit in the operands is 1.

Simple Code Example

```
int flags = 0b00001000;
int enableBit = 0b00000010;
int result = flags | enableBit;   // result is 0b00001010
```

Code Example Explanation

- **Sets a specific bit** in flags without altering other bits.

Notes

- | is useful for setting individual bits in a control register or flag variable.
- Use carefully to avoid unintentionally setting unwanted bits.

Warnings

- Ensure mask values don't unintentionally alter required bits.

3. Bitwise XOR (^)

What is the Bitwise XOR Operator?

The bitwise XOR operator (^) performs a binary XOR operation between corresponding bits of two operands. It's commonly used to toggle specific bits, flipping them from 0 to 1 or from 1 to 0.

Use Purpose

- **Toggling Bits**: Flips specific bits while leaving others unchanged.
- **Clear Bits in a Masked Pattern**: Clears bits based on a predefined pattern.

Syntax

```
result = operand1 ^ operand2;
```

Syntax Explanation

- **result**: Stores the outcome of the bitwise XOR operation.
- **operand1**: The first value.
- **^**: The XOR operator, which sets each bit in result to 1 if the corresponding bits in operand1 and operand2 are different.
- **operand2**: The second value.
- **Operands**: Can be literals, variables, or masks.
- **Result**: Each bit in result is 1 if the bits in the operands differ.

Simple Code Example

```
int state = 0b10101010;
int toggleMask = 0b00000001;
int result = state ^ toggleMask;   // result is 0b10101011
```

Code Example Explanation

- **Toggles the least significant bit** in state, changing it from 0 to 1.

Notes

- ^ is useful for toggling bits, especially in situations where you need to flip specific bits periodically.
- XOR with a bitmask of all 1s (^ 0xFF) inverts all bits in a variable.

4. Bitwise NOT (~)

What is the Bitwise NOT Operator?

The bitwise NOT operator (~) inverts all bits in an operand, changing 1s to 0s and 0s to 1s. This operator is often used to create inverse masks or to toggle all bits in a variable.

Use Purpose

- **Invert All Bits**: Changes each 0 to 1 and each 1 to 0.
- **Create Masks**: Inverts a mask to flip its behavior.

Syntax

```
result = ~operand;
```

Syntax Explanation

- **result**: Stores the inverted value.
- **~**: The NOT operator, which flips each bit in operand.
- **Operand**: Any variable or literal.
- **Result**: All bits in operand are inverted.

Simple Code Example

```
int value = 0b00001111;
int result = ~value;   // result is 0b11110000
```

Code Example Explanation

- **Inverts all bits in value**: Changes each 1 to 0 and each 0 to 1.

Notes

- ~ is often used to create complementary masks.
- Inverts all bits, so it may produce negative values for signed integers.

Warnings

- When working with signed integers, the result may become negative.

5. Left Shift (<<)

What is the Left Shift Operator?

The left shift operator (<<) shifts all bits in a variable to the left by a specified number of positions, filling the empty rightmost bits with 0s. Each shift to the left effectively multiplies the number by 2.

Use Purpose

- **Efficient Multiplication**: Multiplies a number by powers of 2.
- **Position Bits**: Useful for setting specific bit positions.

Syntax

```
result = operand << n;
```

Syntax Explanation

- **result**: Stores the shifted value.
- **operand**: The value to shift.
- **<<**: The left shift operator, which moves bits to the left.
- **n**: The number of positions to shift.
- **Operand**: An integer variable or literal.
- **Result**: operand shifted to the left by n positions.

Simple Code Example

```
int value = 0b00000001;
int result = value << 2;   // result is 0b00000100
```

Code Example Explanation

- **Shifts value two positions left**, multiplying it by 4.

Notes

- Each shift left by 1 position doubles the value.
- Commonly used to set specific bits in a control register.

Warnings

- Shifting too far can lead to overflow, losing significant bits.

6. Right Shift (>>)

What is the Right Shift Operator?

The right shift operator (>>) shifts all bits in a variable to the right by a specified number of positions, filling the leftmost bits with 0s (or with the sign bit in the case of signed integers). Each shift to the right effectively divides the number by 2.

Use Purpose

- **Efficient Division**: Divides a number by powers of 2.
- **Clear Lower Bits**: Useful for isolating high bits in a byte or word.

Syntax

```
result = operand >> n;
```

Syntax Explanation

- **result**: Stores the shifted value.
- **operand**: The value to shift.
- **>>**: The right shift operator, which moves bits to the right.
- **n**: The number of positions to shift.
- **Operand**: An integer variable or literal.
- **Result**: operand shifted to the right by n positions.

Simple Code Example

```
int value = 0b00001000;
int result = value >> 2;   // result is 0b00000010
```

Code Example Explanation

- **Shifts value two positions right**, dividing it by 4.

Notes

- Each shift right by 1 position halves the value.
- Useful for dividing by powers of 2 without using division.

Warnings

- Shifting signed integers may retain the sign bit, leading to unexpected results.

Final Project: LED Pattern Control Using Bitwise Operators

Project Objective

Use bitwise operators to control an 8x8 LED matrix, creating patterns by setting, clearing, and toggling specific bits.

Project Circuit

Component	Pin Description	Connection Details
STM32 Microcontroller	GPIO Output Pins	Controls rows and columns of LED matrix
LED Matrix	8x8 Matrix	Creates display based on bit patterns

Project Code

```c
#include "stm32f4xx_hal.h"
void LED_Matrix_Init(void) {
    // Initialization code for GPIO pins controlling the LED matrix
}
void Set_Row_Pattern(uint8_t row, uint8_t pattern) {
    // Use bitwise operations to control each row's LED pattern
    for (int i = 0; i < 8; i++) {
        if (pattern & (1 << i)) {
            // Set specific column pin high
        } else {
            // Set specific column pin low
        }
    }
}
int main(void) {
    HAL_Init();
    LED_Matrix_Init();

    while (1) {
        Set_Row_Pattern(0, 0b10101010);  // Example row pattern
        HAL_Delay(500);
        Set_Row_Pattern(0, ~0b10101010);  // Invert pattern using NOT
operator
        HAL_Delay(500);
    }
}
```

Save and Run

1. Save the code as `main.c`.
2. Compile and upload to the STM32 NUCLEO-F446RE using STM32CubeIDE or Keil.

Check Output

Expected behavior:

- The LED matrix displays alternating patterns based on bitwise operations, demonstrating bitwise manipulation for visual control.

Summary

This chapter covered essential bitwise operators in C for STM32 programming, including AND, OR, XOR, NOT, left shift, and right shift. These operators are invaluable in embedded systems for manipulating data at the bit level, optimizing memory usage, and controlling hardware directly. The final project demonstrated how to use bitwise operations to control an LED matrix, showcasing practical applications in embedded programming.

Math Functions in STM32

Chapter Overview

Math functions are essential for embedded systems programming, where they play a key role in processing sensor data, controlling outputs, and performing calculations for various applications. The C programming language provides a range of math functions, such as trigonometric, exponential, logarithmic, rounding, and absolute functions, through the standard library (math.h). This chapter covers essential math functions in C, explaining their usage, syntax, and practical applications in STM32 programming.

Chapter Goal

- Understand and apply math functions in C, including square root, power, trigonometric, logarithmic, absolute, rounding, ceiling, and floor functions.
- Use math functions to process and analyze data in embedded systems.
- Implement math functions in a practical project to process sensor data and display results.

Rules

- **Include the Math Library**: Always include math.h at the beginning of your program to access math functions.
- **Be Mindful of Data Types**: Use float or double for functions that return decimal results to avoid type mismatches.
- **Optimize for Efficiency**: Math functions can be computationally intensive, so use them sparingly in time-sensitive applications.
- **Handle Domain Errors**: Ensure inputs are within valid ranges to avoid errors, especially in functions like log() and sqrt().
- **Choose Appropriate Rounding**: Use round(), ceil(), or floor() functions as needed based on your application requirements.

Syntax Table

Serial No	Function	Code Snippet	Simple Example
1	Square Root	`sqrt(x);`	`result = sqrt(16.0);`
2	Power	`pow(base, exponent);`	`result = pow(2, 3);`
3	Sine	`sin(angle);`	`result = sin(3.14159 / 2);`
4	Cosine	`cos(angle);`	`result = cos(0);`
5	Tangent	`tan(angle);`	`result = tan(3.14159 / 4);`
6	Logarithm (base e)	`log(x);`	`result = log(2.71828);`
7	Logarithm (base 10)	`log10(x);`	`result = log10(100);`
8	Absolute Value	`fabs(x);`	`result = fabs(-5.3);`

9	Rounding	`round(x);`	`result = round(3.6);`
10	Ceiling	`ceil(x);`	`result = ceil(2.3);`
11	Floor	`floor(x);`	`result = floor(4.9);`

Topic Explanations

1. Square Root (`sqrt`)

What is the Square Root Function?

The `sqrt` function calculates the square root of a non-negative number. It is commonly used for distance and signal processing calculations in embedded systems.

Use Purpose

- **Distance Calculations**: Computes the Euclidean distance between points.
- **Signal Processing**: Essential for calculating the root mean square (RMS) values in signal analysis.

Syntax

```
result = sqrt(x);
```

Syntax Explanation

- **result**: Stores the square root of x.
- **sqrt**: The square root function.
- **x**: A non-negative number for which to find the square root.

Simple Code Example

```
float value = 16.0;
float result = sqrt(value);   // result is 4.
```

Notes

- x must be non-negative; negative values cause domain errors.
- `sqrt` returns a `double` type.

---

2. Power (pow)

What is the Power Function?

The pow function raises a base to a specified exponent, making it useful for calculations involving exponential growth, scaling, or polynomial equations.

Use Purpose

- **Exponential Growth**: Models data with exponential characteristics.
- **Polynomial Equations**: Evaluates expressions with powers of variables.

Syntax

```
result = pow(base, exponent);
```

Syntax Explanation

- **result**: Stores the value of `base` raised to `exponent`.
- **pow**: The power function.
- **base**: The number to raise.
- **exponent**: The power to raise `base` to.

Simple Code Example

```
float result = pow(2.0, 3.0);  // result is 8.0
```

Notes

- pow works with both positive and negative exponents.
- The result is a `double`.

---

3. Sine (`sin`)

What is the Sine Function?

The `sin` function calculates the sine of an angle (in radians), often used in wave generation and angle calculations in embedded systems.

Use Purpose

- **Wave Generation**: Generates sinusoidal waveforms.
- **Angle Calculations**: Computes the sine of angles for trigonometric applications.

Syntax

```
result = sin(angle);
```

Syntax Explanation

- **result**: Stores the sine of `angle`.
- **sin**: The sine function.
- **angle**: An angle in radians.

Simple Code Example

```
float result = sin(3.14159 / 2);  // result is approximately 1.0
```

Notes

- Angles must be in radians.
- Returns a `double`.

---

4. Cosine (`cos`)

What is the Cosine Function?

The `cos` function calculates the cosine of an angle in radians. It is useful in wave generation, rotations, and angle projections.

Use Purpose

- **Angle Projections**: Calculates projections using cosine of angles.
- **Waveforms**: Generates cosine waveforms for signals.

Syntax

```
result = cos(angle);
```

Syntax Explanation

- **result**: Stores the cosine of `angle`.
- **cos**: The cosine function.
- **angle**: An angle in radians.

Simple Code Example

```
float result = cos(0);  // result is 1.0
```

Notes

- Angles must be in radians.
- Returns a `double`.

---

5. Tangent (`tan`)

What is the Tangent Function?

The `tan` function calculates the tangent of an angle (in radians). It is often used in slope, angle, and wave calculations.

Use Purpose

- **Trigonometric Calculations**: Used for slopes and angle-related calculations.
- **Waveforms**: Useful in generating tangent-based waveforms.

Syntax

```
result = tan(angle);
```

Syntax Explanation

- **result**: Stores the tangent of `angle`.
- **tan**: The tangent function.
- **angle**: An angle in radians.

Simple Code Example

```
float result = tan(3.14159 / 4);  // result is approximately 1.0
```

6. Logarithm (base e) (log)

What is the Logarithm Function?

The log function computes the natural logarithm (base e) of a number. It's useful in scaling, growth, and decay calculations.

Use Purpose

- **Data Scaling**: Converts data to a natural logarithmic scale.
- **Exponential Decay**: Models decay rates.

Syntax

```
result = log(x);
```

Syntax Explanation

- **result**: Stores the natural logarithm of x.
- **log**: The natural logarithm function.
- **x**: A positive number for which to find the logarithm.

Simple Code Example

```
float result = log(2.71828);   // result is approximately 1.0
```

---

7. Logarithm (base 10) (log10)

What is the Logarithm Base 10 Function?

The log10 function calculates the base-10 logarithm of a number, commonly used for decibel calculations and scientific measurements.

Use Purpose

- **Decibel Calculations**: Converts data for logarithmic scales in signal processing.
- **Data Scaling**: Used in scientific data requiring base-10 logarithmic representation.

Syntax

```
result = log10(x);
```

Syntax Explanation

- **result**: Stores the base-10 logarithm of x.

- **log10**: The logarithm base-10 function.
- **x**: A positive number for which to find the base-10 logarithm.

Simple Code Example

```
float result = log10(100);   // result is 2.0
```

8. Absolute Value (fabs)

What is the Absolute Value Function?

The fabs function returns the absolute (non-negative) value of a floating-point number, effectively removing any negative sign.

Use Purpose
- **Magnitude Calculations**: Determines the magnitude of values, regardless of sign.
- **Error Measurements**: Computes absolute error values.

Syntax

```
result = fabs(x);
```

Syntax Explanation
- **result**: Stores the absolute value of x.
- **fabs**: The absolute value function for floating-point numbers.
- **x**: The input value, which may be positive or negative.

Simple Code Example

```
float result = fabs(-5.3);   // result is 5.3
```

9. Rounding (round)

What is the Rounding Function?

The round function rounds a floating-point number to the nearest integer, useful for preparing values for integer-based calculations.

Use Purpose
- **Approximate Calculations**: Rounds floating-point numbers for approximate calculations.
- **Integer Conversion**: Rounds values before casting to integers.

Syntax

```
result = round(x);
```

Syntax Explanation

- **result**: Stores the rounded value of x.
- **round**: The rounding function.
- **x**: The input value, which may have decimals.

Simple Code Example

```
float result = round(3.6);  // result is 4.0
```

10. Ceiling (ceil)

What is the Ceiling Function?

The ceil function returns the smallest integer greater than or equal to a given number, rounding up the value.

Use Purpose

- **Resource Calculations**: Rounds up to ensure adequate resources.
- **Step Calculations**: Rounds values to ensure full step counts.

Syntax

```
result = ceil(x);
```

Syntax Explanation

- **result**: Stores the ceiling of x.
- **ceil**: The ceiling function.
- **x**: The input value.

Simple Code Example

```
float result = ceil(2.3);  // result is 3.0
```

11. Floor (`floor`)

What is the Floor Function?

The `floor` function returns the largest integer less than or equal to a given number, effectively rounding down.

Use Purpose

- **Resource Partitioning**: Rounds down values for partitioning resources without exceeding limits.
- **Lower Bound Rounding**: Ensures calculations stay within a specific limit.

Syntax

```
result = floor(x);
```

Syntax Explanation

- **result**: Stores the floor value of x.
- **floor**: The floor function.
- **x**: The input value.

Simple Code Example

```
float result = floor(4.9);  // result is 4.0
```

Final Project: Sensor Data Processing with Math Functions

Project Name

Real-Time Sensor Data Analysis Using Math Functions

Project Objective

Use math functions to process sensor data, calculate averages, peak values, logarithmic scale, and display the square root of the averaged data.

Project Circuit

Component	Pin Description	Connection Details
STM32 Microcontroller	ADC Channel	Reads data from temperature sensor
Temperature Sensor	Connected to ADC input	Provides temperature data
LCD or Serial Monitor	Display	Shows processed data output

Project Code

```
#include "stm32f4xx_hal.h"
#include <math.h>
#include <stdio.h>

ADC_HandleTypeDef hadc1;

void ADC_Init(void) {
    __HAL_RCC_ADC1_CLK_ENABLE();
    hadc1.Instance = ADC1;
    hadc1.Init.Resolution = ADC_RESOLUTION_12B;
    HAL_ADC_Init(&hadc1);
}

int main(void) {
    HAL_Init();
    ADC_Init();

    uint32_t adcValue;
    float temp, sumTemp = 0, avgTemp, peakTemp = 0;
    int sampleCount = 10;

    for (int i = 0; i < sampleCount; i++) {
        HAL_ADC_Start(&hadc1);
        if (HAL_ADC_PollForConversion(&hadc1, HAL_MAX_DELAY) == HAL_OK)
{
            adcValue = HAL_ADC_GetValue(&hadc1);
            temp = (adcValue * 3.3) / 4095;  // Convert ADC to voltage
            sumTemp += temp;
            if (temp > peakTemp) {
                peakTemp = temp;
            }
        }
    }
```

```
        HAL_Delay(500);
    }

    avgTemp = sumTemp / sampleCount;   // Calculate average
    float rootAvg = sqrt(avgTemp);     // Square root of average
    float logAvg = log10(avgTemp);     // Logarithmic transformation of
average

    printf("Average Temp: %.2f V\n", avgTemp);
    printf("Peak Temp: %.2f V\n", peakTemp);
    printf("Square Root of Avg Temp: %.2f V\n", rootAvg);
    printf("Log10 of Avg Temp: %.2f V\n", logAvg);

    while (1) {}
}
```

Save and Run

1. Save the code as `main.c`.
2. Compile and upload to the STM32 NUCLEO-F446RE using STM32CubeIDE or Keil.

Check Output

Expected behavior:

- The program displays the average temperature, peak temperature, square root of the average, and logarithmic scale of the averaged temperature.

Summary

This chapter covered essential math functions in C for STM32 programming, including square root, power, trigonometric, logarithmic, absolute, rounding, ceiling, and floor functions. These functions enable sophisticated mathematical processing, allowing embedded systems to perform complex calculations. The final project demonstrated the use of these functions to process sensor data, highlighting their importance in data analysis and real-time processing in embedded applications.

Characters in STM32

Chapter Overview

Characters are widely used in embedded systems for text display, user input, and communication. The C programming language provides a range of character functions in the standard library (ctype.h) to classify, convert, and manipulate characters. This chapter covers essential character functions, explaining their usage, syntax, and applications in STM32 programming.

Chapter Goal

- Understand and apply character functions in C, including classification, conversion, and manipulation of characters.
- Learn how to handle characters in embedded systems for communication, display, and input processing.
- Implement character functions in a practical project to process user input or sensor data for display.

Rules

- **Include the Character Library**: Always include ctype.h to access standard character functions.
- **Use Character Functions for Validation**: Validate user input or sensor data with character functions to ensure data integrity.
- **Handle Case Conversion for Uniformity**: Use case conversion functions (toupper() and tolower()) for consistent data handling.
- **Control for Printable and Non-Printable Characters**: Use character classification functions to manage special characters in strings.
- **Use Character Arrays for Strings**: Use character arrays for strings in embedded systems, as C strings are arrays of characters.

Syntax Table

Serial No	Function	Code Snippet	Simple Example
1	Check Digit	`isdigit(c);`	`if (isdigit('5'))` `{ ... }`
2	Check Alphabet	`isalpha(c);`	`if (isalpha('A'))` `{ ... }`
3	Check Alphanumeric	`isalnum(c);`	`if (isalnum('8'))` `{ ... }`
4	Check Lowercase	`islower(c);`	`if (islower('a'))` `{ ... }`
5	Check Uppercase	`isupper(c);`	`if (isupper('B'))` `{ ... }`
6	Convert to Lowercase	`tolower(c);`	`result =` `tolower('A');`
7	Convert to Uppercase	`toupper(c);`	`result =` `toupper('b');`
8	Check Printable	`isprint(c);`	`if (isprint('!'))` `{ ... }`
9	Check Space	`isspace(c);`	`if (isspace(' '))` `{ ... }`

10	Check Hexadecimal	`isxdigit(c);`	`if`
			`(isxdigit('F')) {`
			`... }`

Topic Explanations

1. Check Digit (`isdigit`)

What is the Digit Check Function?

The `isdigit` function checks if a character is a digit (0-9). This is useful for validating numeric input and identifying numeric characters within strings.

Use Purpose

- **Numeric Validation**: Verifies if a character is a digit.
- **Parsing Data**: Helps extract numeric characters from strings.

Syntax

```
if (isdigit(c)) {
    statements;
}
```

Syntax Explanation

- **c**: The character to check.
- **isdigit**: Returns non-zero (true) if c is a digit; otherwise, returns zero (false).

Simple Code Example

```
char c = '5';
if (isdigit(c)) {
    // Character is a digit
}
```

Notes

- Commonly used in loops that validate or parse numeric-only input.
- `isdigit` works only with single characters, not strings.

Warnings

- Avoid using `isdigit` on non-ASCII characters, as results may vary across platforms.
- Check input length beforehand to prevent indexing issues when working with strings.

2. Check Alphabet (`isalpha`)

What is the Alphabet Check Function?

The `isalpha` function checks if a character is an alphabet letter (A-Z, a-z). This is useful for validating alphabetic input and processing letter-based data.

Use Purpose

- **Alphabetic Validation**: Confirms if a character is a letter.
- **Text Processing**: Used to parse alphabetic data in strings.

Syntax

```
if (isalpha(c)) {
    statements;
}
```

Syntax Explanation

- **c**: The character to check.
- **isalpha**: Returns non-zero (true) if c is an alphabet letter; otherwise, returns zero (false).

Simple Code Example

```
char c = 'A';
if (isalpha(c)) {
    // Character is an alphabet letter
}
```

Notes

- Useful for input validation in applications requiring only alphabet characters.
- Works on both uppercase and lowercase characters.

Warnings

- `isalpha` will return false for any non-alphabet characters, so ensure proper handling of spaces or punctuation if needed.
- Be cautious with non-ASCII characters; results may be platform-dependent.

3. Check Alphanumeric (`isalnum`)

What is the Alphanumeric Check Function?

The `isalnum` function checks if a character is alphanumeric, meaning it's either a letter or a digit. This function is useful for ensuring valid alphanumeric input, often used in serial communication and input validation.

Use Purpose

- **Input Validation**: Ensures input is either a letter or a digit.
- **Parsing Mixed Data**: Useful when processing data that contains both letters and numbers.

Syntax

```
if (isalnum(c)) {
    statements;
}
```

Syntax Explanation

- **c**: The character to check.
- **isalnum**: Returns non-zero (true) if c is alphanumeric; otherwise, returns zero (false).

Simple Code Example

```
char c = '9';
if (isalnum(c)) {
    // Character is alphanumeric
}
```

Notes

- Frequently used to parse mixed data formats that exclude symbols and spaces.
- Works well in loop structures that need to filter out non-alphanumeric data.

Warnings

- `isalnum` does not detect special characters, so include additional checks if needed.
- Non-ASCII characters may not be recognized consistently across different platforms.

4. Check Lowercase (`islower`)

What is the Lowercase Check Function?

The `islower` function checks if a character is a lowercase letter (a-z). It is useful for distinguishing between uppercase and lowercase letters, especially in case-sensitive data processing.

Use Purpose

- **Case Detection**: Checks if a character is lowercase.
- **Case Conversion**: Used to selectively convert lowercase characters.

Syntax

```
if (islower(c)) {
    statements;
}
```

Syntax Explanation

- **c**: The character to check.
- **islower**: Returns non-zero (true) if c is a lowercase letter; otherwise, returns zero (false).

Simple Code Example

```
char c = 'g';
if (islower(c)) {
    // Character is lowercase
}
```

Notes

- Use `islower` to process or modify lowercase letters only.
- Works well with text formatting tasks to selectively handle lowercase data.

Warnings

- Avoid using on special characters or non-ASCII characters; results are unreliable.
- Make sure to complement with `isupper` for complete case handling.

5. Check Uppercase (`isupper`)

What is the Uppercase Check Function?

The `isupper` function checks if a character is an uppercase letter (A-Z). It's useful for identifying uppercase letters and converting them if needed.

Use Purpose

- **Case Detection**: Checks if a character is uppercase.
- **Case Conversion**: Helps selectively convert uppercase characters.

Syntax

```
if (isupper(c)) {
    statements;
}
```

Syntax Explanation

- **c**: The character to check.
- **isupper**: Returns non-zero (true) if c is an uppercase letter; otherwise, returns zero (false).

Simple Code Example

```
char c = 'B';
if (isupper(c)) {
    // Character is uppercase
}
```

Notes

- Complements `islower` in applications requiring full case detection.
- Useful in formatting and converting case consistently.

Warnings

- Be cautious of non-ASCII characters; `isupper` may not handle them reliably.
- Avoid assuming input is ASCII-only; add checks if input varies in encoding.

---

6. Convert to Lowercase (`tolower`)

What is the Lowercase Conversion Function?

The `tolower` function converts an uppercase letter to lowercase.
It's commonly used to normalize input, ensuring case consistency.

Use Purpose

- **Case Conversion**: Converts uppercase characters to lowercase.
- **Normalization**: Ensures data is in a consistent case.

Syntax

```
result = tolower(c);
```

Syntax Explanation

- **result**: Stores the lowercase version of c.
- **tolower**: Converts c to lowercase if it's uppercase; otherwise, returns c unchanged.
- **c**: The character to convert.

Simple Code Example

```
char c = 'A';
char result = tolower(c);   // result is 'a'
```

Notes

- Commonly used in data normalization for case-insensitive operations.
- Works well in loops that process multiple characters.

Warnings

- `tolower` will not affect numbers or special characters, so use with `isalpha` for pure alphabet input.
- Avoid using on strings directly; apply character by character.

---

7. Convert to Uppercase (`toupper`)

What is the Uppercase Conversion Function?

The `toupper` function converts a lowercase letter to uppercase, ensuring consistent capitalization.

Use Purpose

- **Case Conversion**: Converts lowercase characters to uppercase.
- **Formatting**: Used to format data with consistent uppercase letters.

Syntax

```
result = toupper(c);
```

Syntax Explanation

- **result**: Stores the uppercase version of c.
- **toupper**: Converts c to uppercase if it's lowercase; otherwise, returns c unchanged.
- **c**: The character to convert.

Simple Code Example

```
char c = 'b';
char result = toupper(c);   // result is 'B'
```

Notes

- Complements `tolower` for case conversion in text-processing applications.
- Useful in standardizing case in user input or communication.

Warnings

- Ensure c is lowercase if conversion is required, as `toupper` won't change numbers or symbols.
- Avoid applying directly to strings; use in loops for each character.

---

8. Check Printable (`isprint`)

What is the Printable Check Function?

The `isprint` function checks if a character is printable, including letters, digits, punctuation, and space, but excluding control characters.

Use Purpose

- **Character Display**: Ensures characters are printable before displaying.
- **Data Validation**: Filters out control characters in strings.

Syntax

```
if (isprint(c)) {
    statements;
}
```

Syntax Explanation

- **c**: The character to check.
- **isprint**: Returns non-zero (true) if c is printable; otherwise, returns zero (false).

Simple Code Example

```
char c = '@';
if (isprint(c)) {
    // Character is printable
}
```

Notes

- Useful for displaying only visible characters in communication tasks.
- Use in loops to filter non-printable characters in received data.

Warnings

- `isprint` returns false for newline (\n) and tab (\t), so check separately if needed.
- Works reliably only with ASCII; handle other encodings with caution.

---

9. Check Space (`isspace`)

What is the Space Check Function?

The `isspace` function checks if a character is a whitespace character, such as a space, tab, or newline.

Use Purpose

- **Whitespace Management**: Identifies whitespace for string processing.
- **Input Parsing**: Useful for handling spaces in input strings.

Syntax

```
if (isspace(c)) {
    statements;
}
```

Syntax Explanation

- **c**: The character to check.
- **isspace**: Returns non-zero (true) if c is a whitespace character; otherwise, returns zero (false).

Simple Code Example

```
char c = ' ';
if (isspace(c)) {
    // Character is whitespace
}
```

Notes

- Useful for ignoring spaces in input processing or user input validation.
- Helps in parsing strings by detecting spaces between words.

Warnings

- isspace will return true for all whitespace characters, not just spaces.
- Handle \n and \t explicitly if required for your application.

---

10. Check Hexadecimal (isxdigit)

What is the Hexadecimal Check Function?

The isxdigit function checks if a character is a hexadecimal digit (0-9, A-F, a-f), often used when parsing hexadecimal data.

Use Purpose

- **Hexadecimal Parsing**: Identifies valid hexadecimal characters in strings.
- **Data Validation**: Ensures characters in hexadecimal data are valid.

Syntax

```
if (isxdigit(c)) {
    statements;
}
```

Syntax Explanation

- **c**: The character to check.
- **isxdigit**: Returns non-zero (true) if c is a hexadecimal digit; otherwise, returns zero (false).

Simple Code Example

```
char c = 'F';
if (isxdigit(c)) {
    // Character is a hexadecimal digit
}
```

Notes

- Useful in processing hex values from user input or communication.
- Complements functions that handle conversion from hexadecimal.

Warnings

- Ensure c is single-character input, as `isxdigit` only works on one character.
- Avoid using on entire strings without looping, as it will only check the first character.

Final Project: Character Processing in Serial Communication

Project Objective

Process serial data using character functions to validate input, convert cases, and extract alphanumeric characters for display or further processing.**Project Circuit**

Component	Pin Description	Connection Details
STM32 Microcontroller	UART Pins	Receives data from serial input
Serial Monitor	UART Communication	Displays processed data

Project Code

```c
#include "stm32f4xx_hal.h"
#include <ctype.h>
#include <stdio.h>
UART_HandleTypeDef huart1;

void UART_Init(void) {
    __HAL_RCC_USART1_CLK_ENABLE();
    huart1.Instance = USART1;
    huart1.Init.BaudRate = 9600;
    huart1.Init.WordLength = UART_WORDLENGTH_8B;
    huart1.Init.StopBits = UART_STOPBITS_1;
    huart1.Init.Parity = UART_PARITY_NONE;
    huart1.Init.Mode = UART_MODE_TX_RX;
    HAL_UART_Init(&huart1);
}
void Process_Character(char c) {
    if (isalpha(c)) {
        c = tolower(c);   // Convert to lowercase
        printf("Alpha character: %c\n", c);
    } else if (isdigit(c)) {
        printf("Digit character: %c\n", c);
    } else if (isspace(c)) {
        printf("Whitespace detected.\n");
    } else if (isprint(c)) {
        printf("Printable symbol: %c\n", c);
    } else {
        printf("Non-printable character received.\n");
    }
}
int main(void) {
    HAL_Init();
    UART_Init();

    char received;
    while (1) {
        if (HAL_UART_Receive(&huart1, (uint8_t*)&received, 1,
HAL_MAX_DELAY) == HAL_OK) {
            Process_Character(received);
        }
    }
}
```

Save and Run

1. Save the code as `main.c`.
2. Compile and upload to the STM32 NUCLEO-F446RE using STM32CubeIDE or Keil.

Check Output

Based on the received character, the program will output the character type and converted case where applicable, displaying information on the serial monitor.

Random Numbers in STM32

Chapter Overview

Random number generation is widely used in embedded systems for applications like data simulation, randomized testing, and game development. In C programming, the standard library provides functions to generate pseudo-random numbers. Although true random number generation is limited on STM32 microcontrollers, we can use functions to create repeatable pseudo-random sequences suitable for most embedded applications. This chapter covers the essential functions for generating random numbers, seeding the random number generator, and applying random numbers within STM32 projects.

Chapter Goal

- Understand and use the main functions for generating random numbers in C.
- Learn how to initialize the random number generator with a seed value.
- Apply random numbers in a practical project to simulate sensor data.

Rules

- **Use srand to Seed the Generator**: Always initialize the random number generator with srand to produce different random sequences on each run.
- **Apply a Seed Based on Time**: For a new random sequence in each execution, use a varying seed, such as the system time.
- **Understand the Range of rand**: The rand function generates numbers from 0 to RAND_MAX, so apply modulo or scaling to restrict the range.
- **Use Pseudo-Random Sequences**: Recognize that rand produces pseudo-random numbers, suitable for most embedded applications but not for cryptographic purposes.

- **Optimize Random Usage in Real-Time Applications**: Avoid overuse of random functions in timing-critical code to maintain performance.

Syntax Table

Serial No	Function	Code Snippet	Simple Example
1	Seed Random Number	`srand(seed);`	`srand(time(NULL));`
2	Generate Random Number	`rand();`	`int randomNumber = rand();`
3	Random in Range	`(rand() % range) + min;`	`int randomInRange = (rand() % 10) + 1;`

Topic Explanations

1. Seed Random Number (`srand`)

What is the Seed Random Number Function?

The `srand` function initializes the random number generator with a seed value, making the random number sequence different on each program execution. Without setting a seed, `rand` generates the same sequence every time the program runs, which can be useful in debugging but may not be desirable in many applications.

Use Purpose
- **Randomize Sequence**: Seeds the generator for different random sequences on each run.
- **Controlled Random Sequences**: Use a fixed seed for repeatable pseudo-random sequences.

Syntax

```
srand(seed);
```

Syntax Explanation

- **srand**: Function that seeds the random number generator.
- **seed**: The value to initialize the random number sequence. A common choice is `time(NULL)`, which uses the current system time.

Simple Code Example

```
#include <stdlib.h>
#include <time.h>

srand(time(NULL));  // Seeds random generator with current time
```

Code Example Explanation

- **Uses the current time as the seed**: Each execution generates a different random sequence based on the time of day.

Notes

- Always seed the generator with `srand` before calling `rand` to avoid generating the same sequence.
- Use a constant seed (like `srand(1)`) if you need the same random sequence each time.

Warnings

- Calling `srand` multiple times within the same program can reset the sequence unpredictably; call it once at the beginning of the program.

---

2. Generate Random Number (rand)

What is the Random Number Generation Function?

The `rand` function generates a pseudo-random integer between 0 and RAND_MAX. RAND_MAX is defined in `stdlib.h` and is often 32767, but it may vary depending on the system.

Use Purpose

- **Basic Random Generation**: Generates a pseudo-random number in a fixed range.
- **Data Simulation**: Useful for simulating sensor data, testing algorithms, and creating random behavior.

Syntax

```
int randomValue = rand();
```

Syntax Explanation

- **rand**: Function that generates a pseudo-random integer.
- **randomValue**: Stores the generated random number.
- **Return Range**: The value is between 0 and RAND_MAX.

Simple Code Example

```
#include <stdlib.h>

int randomNumber = rand();  // Generates a random integer
```

Code Example Explanation

- **Generates a random integer**: The result is a pseudo-random value between 0 and RAND_MAX.

Notes

- Calling rand without srand generates the same sequence each run, so always seed with srand first.
- Use modulo arithmetic with rand to limit the result to a specific range.

---

3. Generate Random Number in a Specific Range

What is the Random Range Function?

By using modulo and offset with rand, you can generate random numbers within a specified range. This is useful in applications where you need a specific minimum and maximum value, such as generating temperatures or positions.

Use Purpose

- **Limit Range**: Produces random values within a specified minimum and maximum range.
- **Simulation Control**: Used in simulation to generate values that fit specific requirements.

Syntax

```
int randomInRange = (rand() % range) + min;
```

Syntax Explanation

- **rand() % range**: Limits the random number to `range` possible values (0 to `range` - 1).
- **+ min**: Shifts the result to start at `min`.
- **Operands**: `range` is the size of the range, and `min` is the minimum value of the range.

Simple Code Example

```
#include <stdlib.h>
#include <time.h>

srand(time(NULL));
int randomInRange = (rand() % 10) + 1;   // Generates a random number
between 1 and 10
```

Code Example Explanation

- **Generates a random number between 1 and 10**: The modulo limits the result to 10 possible values, and adding 1 shifts it to the range of 1–10.

Notes

- Adjust `range` and `min` as needed for other specific ranges.
- Useful for simulating specific data ranges, like sensor values or game positions.

Final Project: Randomized Sensor Data Simulation

Simulate temperature data from a sensor by generating random values within a realistic range. Display the random temperature data periodically to simulate a real-time sensor reading.

Project Circuit

Component	Pin Description	Connection Details
STM32 Microcontroller	GPIO Output or Serial Port	Sends random temperature data
LCD or Serial Monitor	Display	Shows simulated temperature data

Project Code

```
#include "stm32f4xx_hal.h"
#include <stdlib.h>
#include <time.h>
#include <stdio.h>
void SystemClock_Config(void);
int main(void) {
    HAL_Init();
    SystemClock_Config();
    srand(time(NULL));   // Seed random number generator with current
time
    while (1) {
        int randomTemperature = (rand() % 50) + 10;   // Generates
temperature between 10°C and 60°C
        printf("Simulated Temperature: %d°C\n", randomTemperature);   //
Display simulated temperature
        HAL_Delay(1000);   // Delay 1 second to simulate periodic sensor
reading
    }
}
// System Clock Configuration function
void SystemClock_Config(void) {
    // Configuration code to set up the system clock
}
```

Save and Run

1. Save the code as main.c.
2. Compile and upload to the STM32 NUCLEO-F446RE using STM32CubeIDE or Keil.

Check Output

- The serial monitor or display shows a simulated temperature value between 10°C and 60°C every second, demonstrating random number generation within a specified range.

Printing Output in STM32

Chapter Overview

Printing output is essential for debugging, testing, and displaying data in embedded systems. Unlike general-purpose computers, microcontrollers often lack built-in display interfaces, so output is usually printed via serial communication to a terminal. The `printf` function in C can be used with serial communication libraries to display information on a serial monitor. This chapter covers setting up `printf` for serial output, using `printf` formatting, and debugging techniques for STM32.

Chapter Goal

- Learn how to configure `printf` for serial communication on STM32 microcontrollers.
- Understand different `printf` formatting options for various data types.
- Use `printf` for debugging and displaying real-time data from sensors or other sources.

Rules

- **Redirect `printf` to Serial Port**: Use the `HAL_UART_Transmit` function to send `printf` output to a serial port.
- **Use Format Specifiers Appropriately**: Ensure the format specifier matches the data type being printed.
- **Set Baud Rate Correctly**: Match the baud rate in the serial monitor with the STM32's UART configuration.
- **Buffer Output Carefully**: Use buffers to handle and format strings before sending data.
- **Limit Printing in Real-Time Loops**: Excessive printing can slow down real-time applications, so limit the frequency of output.

Syntax Table

Serial No	Function	Code Snippet	Simple Example
1	Print Integer	`printf("%d", integer);`	`printf("Value: %d\n", 25);`
2	Print Float	`printf("%f", floatValue);`	`printf("Temperature : %.2f\n", 25.3);`
3	Print Character	`printf("%c", character);`	`printf("Letter: %c\n", 'A');`
4	Print String	`printf("%s", string);`	`printf("Hello, %s\n", "World");`
5	Print Hexadecimal	`printf("%x", hexValue);`	`printf("Hex: %x\n", 255);`

Topic Explanations

1. Configuring `printf` for Serial Communication

What is Serial Communication with `printf`?

The `printf` function in C, typically used for console output, can be redirected to a UART (serial port) to display output on a terminal monitor. This configuration is essential for STM32 microcontrollers, as they lack native display interfaces. The output can be viewed on a connected computer through a serial terminal (such as PuTTY or the Serial Monitor in STM32CubeIDE).

Use Purpose

- **Display Output**: Send values, messages, and debugging information to a serial terminal.
- **Debugging**: Print sensor values, loop counts, and error codes to diagnose issues.

Syntax

```
int _write(int file, char *ptr, int len) {
    HAL_UART_Transmit(&huart2, (uint8_t*)ptr, len, HAL_MAX_DELAY);
    return len;
}
```

Syntax Explanation

- **_write**: The function that `printf` calls internally to write output.
- **file**: Ignored for standard `printf` output in embedded systems.
- **ptr**: The pointer to the string being printed.
- **len**: The length of the string.
- **HAL_UART_Transmit**: Transmits data over UART, with &huart2 specifying the UART handle (adjustable based on your configuration).
- **len**: Returns the number of characters sent.

Simple Code Example

```
#include "stm32f4xx_hal.h"
#include <stdio.h>

UART_HandleTypeDef huart2;

int _write(int file, char *ptr, int len) {
    HAL_UART_Transmit(&huart2, (uint8_t*)ptr, len, HAL_MAX_DELAY);
    return len;
}

int main(void) {
    HAL_Init();
    // UART2 initialization here (baud rate, GPIO config)
    printf("Hello, STM32!\n");
}
```

Code Example Explanation

- **Configures `printf` for UART2**: Redirects `printf` output to UART2.
- **Prints "Hello, STM32!"**: Displays the text on the connected serial monitor.

Notes

- Set up the UART with the desired baud rate, typically 9600 or 115200 bps.
- _write is called by printf to send data through UART.

Warnings

- Ensure that UART configuration (baud rate, stop bits) matches the terminal settings.

---

2. Print Integer (%d)

What is Integer Printing?

Using %d in printf prints an integer value in decimal format. Integers are often used to represent discrete values like sensor readings or status codes.

Use Purpose

- **Display Values**: Print integer values like counts, IDs, and statuses.
- **Debugging**: Observe integer values to check program flow or verify calculations.

Syntax

```
printf("%d", integer);
```

Syntax Explanation

- **%d**: Format specifier for printing integers.
- **integer**: The variable containing the integer to print.

Simple Code Example

```
int value = 25;
printf("Value: %d\n", value);   // Prints "Value: 25"
```

Code Example Explanation

- **Displays the integer value of value**: Outputs 25 in decimal format.

Notes

- %d is for signed integers; use %u for unsigned integers.

Warnings

- Mismatched format specifiers and data types can lead to incorrect output.

---

3. Print Float (%f)

What is Float Printing?

Using %f in `printf` displays a floating-point number. Floats are commonly used for decimal values, such as sensor readings and calculated results.

Use Purpose

- **Display Measurements**: Print values with decimal precision, like temperature or voltage.
- **Debugging Calculations**: Display results of calculations with fractional values.

Syntax

```
printf("%f", floatValue);
```

Syntax Explanation

- **%f**: Format specifier for printing floating-point values.
- **floatValue**: The variable containing the floating-point number to print.

Simple Code Example

```
float temperature = 25.3;
printf("Temperature: %.2f\n", temperature);  // Prints "Temperature: 25.30"
```

Code Example Explanation

- **Prints `temperature` to two decimal places**: Outputs 25.30 with specified precision.

Notes
- Use %.2f to print to two decimal places.
- STM32 may require enabling float printing in the standard library.

Warnings
- Floating-point printing may slow down real-time applications.

---

4. Print Character (%c)

What is Character Printing?

Using %c in printf prints a single character. This is useful for displaying individual symbols or ASCII values in embedded systems.

Use Purpose
- **Display Characters**: Print single characters or control characters.
- **Debugging**: Useful for observing ASCII values or debugging text parsing.

Syntax

```
printf("%c", character);
```

Syntax Explanation
- **%c**: Format specifier for printing a character.
- **character**: The variable containing the character to print.

Simple Code Example

```
char letter = 'A';
printf("Letter: %c\n", letter);   // Prints "Letter: A"
```

Code Example Explanation
- **Displays letter as a character**: Outputs A to the terminal.

Notes
- char type is often used for single characters or ASCII values.

Warnings
- Ensure the variable is of char type to avoid incorrect output.

5. Print String (%s)

What is String Printing?

Using %s in `printf` displays a string, which is a series of characters. Strings are often used for output messages, prompts, and displaying sensor names.

Use Purpose

- **Display Messages**: Print prompts, names, and strings of text.
- **User Interface**: Provides feedback to users in a readable format.

Syntax

```
printf("%s", string);
```

Syntax Explanation

- **%s**: Format specifier for printing a string.
- **string**: A pointer to the string of characters to print.

Simple Code Example

```
char name[] = "STM32";
printf("Hello, %s!\n", name);   // Prints "Hello, STM32!"
```

Code Example Explanation

- **Displays name**: Outputs Hello, STM32! to the terminal.

Notes

- Strings must be null-terminated (\0) to print correctly.

Warnings

- Ensure the string is properly null-terminated to avoid undefined behavior.

6. Print Hexadecimal (%x)

What is Hexadecimal Printing?

Using %x in `printf` displays an integer value in hexadecimal format. Hexadecimal output is useful for debugging memory addresses, flags, and binary data.

Use Purpose

- **Memory and Debugging**: Displays values in a compact, hexadecimal format.
- **Display Addresses**: Print memory addresses, which are usually in hexadecimal.

Syntax

```
printf("%x", hexValue);
```

Syntax Explanation

- **%x**: Format specifier for printing hexadecimal values.
- **hexValue**: The integer variable to print as hexadecimal.

Simple Code Example

```
int hexValue = 255;
printf("Hex: %x\n", hexValue);  // Prints "Hex: ff"
```

Code Example Explanation

- **Prints hexValue in hexadecimal format**: Outputs ff as hexadecimal for 255.

Notes

- Use 0x%x to prefix with 0x for clearer hexadecimal display.

Warnings

- Mismatched format specifiers can result in incorrect output.

Final Project: Displaying Sensor Data with `printf`

Project Objective

Collect data from a temperature sensor and display it over UART using `printf`. This project demonstrates using different `printf` format specifiers to print temperature values and system messages on a serial terminal.

Component	Pin Description	Connection Details
STM32 Microcontroller	UART TX	Connects to the serial monitor
Temperature Sensor	Analog Input	Provides temperature data
Serial Monitor	USB UART	Displays temperature data output

Project Code

```c
#include "stm32f4xx_hal.h"
#include <stdio.h>

UART_HandleTypeDef huart2;

int _write(int file, char *ptr, int len) {
    HAL_UART_Transmit(&huart2, (uint8_t*)ptr, len, HAL_MAX_DELAY);
    return len;
}

void SystemClock_Config(void);
void UART2_Init(void);

int main(void) {
    HAL_Init();
    SystemClock_Config();
    UART2_Init();

    printf("Temperature Sensor Monitoring\n");

    while (1) {
        float temperature = 25.3;  // Placeholder for actual sensor
reading
        printf("Current Temperature: %.2f°C\n", temperature);
        HAL_Delay(1000);  // Print temperature every second
    }
}

// Initialize UART2
void UART2_Init(void) {
    huart2.Instance = USART2;
    huart2.Init.BaudRate = 9600;
    huart2.Init.WordLength = UART_WORDLENGTH_8B;
    huart2.Init.StopBits = UART_STOPBITS_1;
    huart2.Init.Parity = UART_PARITY_NONE;
    huart2.Init.Mode = UART_MODE_TX_RX;
    HAL_UART_Init(&huart2);
}
```

```
// System Clock Configuration function
void SystemClock_Config(void) {
    // Configuration code for system clock
}
```

Save and Run

1. Save the code as main.c.
2. Compile and upload to the STM32 NUCLEO-F446RE using STM32CubeIDE or Keil.

Check Output

Expected behavior:

- The serial monitor displays a message followed by temperature readings every second, formatted using printf.

www.ingramcontent.com/pod-product-compliance
Lightning Source LLC
LaVergne TN
LVHW051327050326
832903LV00031B/3407